# Chambers
# German
# Grammar

Chambers

CHAMBERS
An imprint of Chambers Harrap Publishers Ltd
7 Hopetoun Crescent, Edinburgh, EH7 4AY

Chambers Harrap is an Hachette UK company

© Chambers Harrap Publishers Ltd 2009

Chambers® is a registered trademark of Chambers Harrap Publishers Ltd

This third edition published by Chambers Harrap Publishers Ltd 2009
First published as *Harrap's German Grammar* in 1988
Second edition published 2003

The moral rights of the author have been asserted
Database right Chambers Harrap Publishers Ltd (makers)

All rights reserved. No part of this publication may be reproduced, stored in a
retrieval system, or transmitted in any form or by any means, electronic, mechanical,
photocopying, recording or otherwise, without the prior permission in writing of
Chambers Harrap Publishers Ltd, or as expressly permitted by law, or under terms
agreed with the appropriate reprographics rights organization. Enquiries concerning
reproduction outside the scope of the above should be sent to the Rights Department,
Chambers Harrap Publishers Ltd, at the address above.

You must not circulate this book in any other binding or cover and you must impose
this same condition on any acquirer.

A CIP catalogue record for this book is available from the British Library.

ISBN 978 0550 10506 6

10 9 8 7 6 5 4 3 2 1

We have made every effort to mark as such all words which we believe to be
trademarks. We should also like to make it clear that the presence of a word in the
book, whether marked or unmarked, in no way affects its legal status as a trademark.

Every reasonable effort has been made by the author and the publishers to trace the
copyright holders of material quoted in this book. Any errors or omissions should be
notified in writing to the publishers, who will endeavour to rectify the situation for
any reprints and future editions.

Project Editors: Alex Hepworth, Kate Nicholson
With Helen Bleck

www.chambers.co.uk


Designed by Chambers Harrap Publishers Ltd, Edinburgh
Typeset in Rotis Serif and Meta Plus by Macmillan Publishing Solutions
Printed and bound in Spain by Graphy Cems

# CONTENTS

# CONTENTS

# INTRODUCTION

This German grammar from Chambers has been written to meet
the needs of all students of German, and is particularly suited for
those taking school examinations. The essential rules of the German
language have been explained in terms that are as accessible as
possible to all users. Where technical terms have been used then full
explanations of these terms have also been supplied. There is also a
full glossary of grammatical terminology on pages 7-14.

While literary aspects of the German language have not been
ignored, the emphasis has been placed squarely on modern spoken
German. This grammar, with its wealth of lively and typical
illustrations of usage taken from the present-day language, is the
ideal study aid for all levels – from the beginner who is starting
to get to grips with the German language through to the advanced
user who requires a comprehensive and readily accessible work of
reference. All the changes due to the German spelling reforms have
been integrated into the text.

For this new edition the text has been fully revised and updated,
while the smart new two-colour design makes consultation even
easier and more enjoyable.

*Abbreviations used in the text:*

| | |
|---|---|
| *acc* | accusative |
| *dat* | dative |
| *fem* | feminine |
| *gen* | genitive |
| *indef art* | indefinite article |
| *masc* | masculine |
| *neut* | neuter |
| *nom* | nominative |
| *pl* | plural |
| *pron* | pronoun |
| *sing* | singular |

# 1 GLOSSARY OF GRAMMATICAL TERMS

**ABSTRACT**   An abstract noun is one which names a quality or a concept rather than a concrete physical object or a person. Examples of abstract nouns are **happiness, life, length**.

**ACCUSATIVE**   The accusative is the case used when a noun or pronoun (and any related article and adjective) is the object of a verb. For example, in the phrases **I love him/this old city** the words *him* and *this old city* are objects and, in German, must be put in the accusative case. It is also used after certain prepositions, eg **für mich** (for me).

**ACTIVE**   The active form of a verb is the basic form as in **I remember her**. It is normally opposed to the PASSIVE form of the verb as in **she will be remembered**.

**ADJECTIVAL NOUN**   An adjectival noun is an adjective used as a noun. For example, the adjective *young* is used as a noun in **the young at heart**.

**ADJECTIVE**   A describing word telling us what something or someone is like (eg **a *small* house, the *Royal* Family, an *interesting* pastime**).

**ADVERB**   Adverbs are normally used with a verb to add extra information by indicating *how* the action is done (adverbs of manner), *when*, *where* and *with how much intensity* the action is done (adverbs of time, place and intensity), or *to what extent* the action is done (adverbs of quantity). Adverbs may also be used with an adjective or another adverb (eg **a *very* attractive girl, *very* well**).

**AGREEMENT** In German, words such as adjectives, articles and pronouns are said to agree in number, gender and case with the noun or pronoun they refer to. This means that their form changes according to the **number** of the noun (singular or plural), its **gender** (masculine, feminine or neuter) and its **case** (nominative, accusative, genitive or dative).

**APPOSITION** A word or phrase is said to be in apposition to another when it is placed directly after it without any joining word (eg Mr Jones, **our bank manager**, rang today).

**ARTICLE** *See* DEFINITE ARTICLE *and* INDEFINITE ARTICLE.

**AUXILIARY** Auxiliary verbs are used to form compound tenses of other verbs, eg **have** in I **have** seen or **will** in she **will** go. The main auxiliary verbs in German are sein, haben and werden.

**CARDINAL** Cardinal numbers are numbers such as **one, two, ten, fourteen**, as opposed to ORDINAL numbers (eg **first, second**).

**CASE** German has four cases (*see* NOMINATIVE, ACCUSATIVE, GENITIVE, DATIVE). Each case is indicated by the endings of nouns, adjectives and articles, and the forms or endings of pronouns.

**CLAUSE** A clause is a group of words which contains at least a subject and a verb: **he said** is a clause. A clause often contains more than this basic information, eg **he said this to her yesterday**. Sentences can be made up of several clauses, eg **he said/he'd call me/if he were free**. *See* SENTENCE.

**COLLECTIVE** A collective noun is one which names a group of people or things but which is singular in form. Examples of collective nouns are **flock** or **fleet**.

**COLLOQUIAL** Colloquial language is the sort of language that can be used in everyday informal conversation, but is avoided in formal writing such as business letters, legal documents *etc*.

**COMPARATIVE** The comparative forms of adjectives and adverbs are used to compare two things, persons or actions. In English, more ... than, -er than, less ... than and as ... as are used for comparison.

**COMPLEMENT** The complement is the part of the clause which completes the information on the subject. It may be a noun group (That is *a very difficult question,* She'll make *a good leader*), an adjective group (You seem *tired and stressed*) or a prepositional phrase, that is, a preposition plus a noun group (The cat is *in the garden*).

**COMPOUND** Compound tenses are verb tenses consisting of more than one element. In German, the compound tenses of a verb are formed by the AUXILIARY verb and the PAST PARTICIPLE and/ or INFINITIVE: ich habe gesehen, er ist gekommen, er wird kommen.

**COMPOUND NOUNS** Compound nouns are nouns made up of two or more separate words. English examples are goalkeeper or dinner party. German compound nouns are normally written as a single word.

**CONDITIONAL** This mood is used to describe what someone would do, or something that would happen if a condition were fulfilled (eg I *would come* if I was well; the chair *would have broken* if he had sat on it).

**CONJUGATION** The conjugation of a verb is the set of different forms taken in the particular tenses and moods of that verb.

**CONJUNCTION** Conjunctions are linking words (eg and, but, or). They may be subordinating or coordinating. Coordinating conjunctions are words like und, aber, oder; subordinating conjunctions are words like weil, wenn, obgleich.

**DATIVE** The dative is the case used in German when a noun or pronoun (and any related article and adjective) is the indirect object of a verb. For example, in ich habe es ihm gegeben ('I gave it to him'), the word ihm is in the dative case. The dative is also used after certain prepositions, eg mit mir ('with me').

**DECLENSION** The declension of nouns and adjectives is the name given to the system of endings that they take.

**DEFINITE ARTICLE** The definite article is the in English and der, die, das in German.

**DEMONSTRATIVE** Demonstrative adjectives (eg this, that, these) and pronouns (eg this one, that one) are used to point out a particular person or thing.

**DIRECT OBJECT** This is a noun or a pronoun which in English follows a verb without any linking preposition, eg I met a *friend*. In German the direct object is always in the accusative case. (Note that in English a preposition is often omitted, eg I sent him a present: *him* is the equivalent of *to him*; *a present* is the direct object).

**ENDING** The ending of a verb is determined by the PERSON (1st/2nd/3rd) and NUMBER (singular/plural) of its subject. In German, nouns also have endings depending on their number and case.

**EXCLAMATION.** Words or phrases used to express surprise, annoyance *etc* (eg what!, wow!, how lucky!, what a nice day!).

**FEMININE** *See* GENDER

**FINITE** The finite verb is the form which has the endings indicating person and tense.

**GENDER**   The gender of a noun indicates whether the noun is *masculine*, *feminine* or *neuter*. In German, the gender of a noun is not always determined by the sex of what it refers to, eg das Mädchen ('the girl') is a neuter noun.

**GENITIVE**   The genitive case is used in German when some form of possession is being expressed, normally equivalent to the English use of the word **of**. For example, in the phrase **the colour of the car**, the words *of the car* must be in the genitive case in German.

**IDIOM**   Idioms, or idiomatic expressions, are phrases which cannot normally be translated word for word. For example, **it's raining cats and dogs** is translated by es regnet Bindfäden.

**IMPERATIVE**   A mood used for giving orders (eg **stop!**, **don't go!**) or for making suggestions (eg **let's go**).

**INDEFINITE**   Indefinite pronouns are words that do not refer to a definite person or object (eg **each**, **someone**).

**INDEFINITE ARTICLE**   The indefinite article is **a** in English and ein, eine, einen *etc* in German.

**INDICATIVE**   The normal form of a verb as in **I like**, **he came**, **we are trying**. It used for asking questions and making statements, and is opposed to the subjunctive, conditional and imperative.

**INDIRECT OBJECT**   This is a pronoun or noun which follows a verb sometimes with a linking preposition (usually **to**), eg **I spoke to** *my friend/him*, **she gave** *him* **a kiss**. In German the indirect object takes the dative case.

**INFINITIVE**   The infinitive is the form of the verb as found in dictionaries. Thus **to eat**, **to finish**, **to take** are infinitives. In German, all infinitives end in -n: leben, gehen, lächeln, ärgern.

**INTERROGATIVE** Interrogative words are used to ask a QUESTION. This may be a direct question (*when* will you arrive?) or an indirect question (I don't know *when* he'll arrive).

**MASCULINE** *See* GENDER

**MOOD** The name given to the four main areas within which a verb is conjugated. *See* INDICATIVE, SUBJUNCTIVE, CONDITIONAL, IMPERATIVE.

**NEUTER** *See* GENDER

**NOMINATIVE** The nominative case is the case used when a noun or pronoun (and any related article and adjectives) is the subject of a verb, eg in the phrase the new caretaker speaks German, the words *the new caretaker* must be in the nominative case in German.

**NOUN** A naming word, which can refer to living creatures, things, people, places or abstract ideas, eg postman, cat, shop, Germany, life.

**NUMBER** The number of a noun indicates whether the noun is SINGULAR or PLURAL. A singular noun refers to one single thing or person (eg boy, train) and a plural noun to several (eg boys, trains).

**OBJECT** *See* DIRECT OBJECT, INDIRECT OBJECT

**ORDINAL** Ordinal numbers are first, second, third, fourth *etc*. In German, all ordinal numbers end in -te(r/s).

**PASSIVE** A verb is used in the passive when the subject of the verb does not perform the action but is subjected to it. In English, the passive is formed with a part of the verb to be and the past participle of the verb, eg he was rewarded. It is used in contrast to the ACTIVE.

**PAST PARTICIPLE** The past participle of a verb is the form which is used after **to have** in English to form the past tense, eg I have **eaten**, I have **said**, you have **tried**.

**PERSON** In any tense, there are three persons in the singular (1st: I ..., 2nd: you ..., 3rd: he/she/it ...), and three in the plural (1st: we ..., 2nd: you ..., 3rd: they ...). *See also* ENDING.

**PERSONAL PRONOUNS** Personal pronouns stand for a noun. In English they are words like **I, you, he/she/it, we, they** or **me, you, him/her/it, us, them**.

**PLURAL** *See* NUMBER

**POSSESSIVE** Possessives are used to indicate possession or ownership. They are words like **my/mine, your/yours, our/ours**.

**PREPOSITION** Prepositions are words such as **with, in, to, at**. They are normally followed by a noun or a pronoun.

**PRESENT PARTICIPLE** The present participle is the verb form which ends in **-ing** in English (**-end** in German).

**PRONOUN** A word which stands for a noun. The main categories of pronouns are:

* Personal pronouns (eg **you, him, us**)
* Possessive pronouns (eg **mine, yours, his**)
* Reflexive pronouns (eg **myself, himself**)
* Interrogative pronouns (eg **who?, what?, which?**)
* Relative pronouns (eg **who, which, that**)
* Demonstrative pronouns (eg **this, that, these**)
* Indefinite pronouns (eg **something, none**)

**QUESTION** There are two question forms: *direct* questions stand on their own and require a question mark at the end (eg **when** will he come?); *indirect* questions are introduced by a clause and require no question mark (eg **I wonder** when he will come).

**REFLEXIVE** Reflexive verbs 'reflect' the action back onto the subject (eg I dressed *myself*). They are always found with a reflexive pronoun and are much more common in German than in English.

**SENTENCE** A sentence is a group of words made up of one or more clauses (*see* CLAUSE). The end of a sentence is indicated by a punctuation mark (usually a full stop, a question mark or an exclamation mark).

**SINGULAR** *See* NUMBER

**STEM** *See* VERB STEM

**SUBJECT** The subject of a verb is the noun or pronoun which performs the action. In the sentences *the train left early* and *she bought a record, the train* and *she* are the subjects.

**SUBJUNCTIVE** The subjunctive is a verb form used to express wishes, doubts and possibilities which is rarely used in English (eg if I *were* you, God *save* the Queen). It is more common in German.

**SUPERLATIVE** The form of an adjective or an adverb which, in English, is marked by the most ..., the -est or the least ....

**TENSE** Verbs are used in tenses, which indicate when an action takes place, eg in the present, the past, the future.

**VERB** A 'doing' word, which usually describes an action (eg to sing, to work, to watch). Some verbs describe a state (eg to be, to have, to hope).

**VERB STEM** The stem of a verb is its 'basic unit' to which the various endings are added. To find the stem of a German verb remove -en or -n from the infinitive. The stem of sagen is sag, the stem of ärgern is ärger.

**VOICE** The two voices of a verb are its ACTIVE and PASSIVE forms.

# **2 ARTICLES**

The form of any article depends on whether the noun following it is masculine, feminine or neuter, whether it is singular or plural and which case it is in.

## A THE DEFINITE ARTICLE

### **1** Forms

a) The definite article in English has only one form – 'the'.

The definite article in German changes its ending according to the gender and case of the noun, and whether it is singular or plural. For the use of the cases, *see* pp 51-3.

|  | **MASCULINE** | **FEMININE** | **NEUTER** | **PLURAL ALL GENDERS** |
|---|---|---|---|---|
| *nom* | der | die | das | die |
| *acc* | den | die | das | die |
| *gen* | des | der | des | der |
| *dat* | dem | der | dem | den |

**die Lehrerin kommt später**
the teacher's coming later

**hier sind die Äpfel**
here are the apples

**kennst du den Sänger?**
do you know the singer?

**es steht auf dem Tisch**
it's on the table

**der Anfang des Liedes**
the beginning of the song

**sag es den anderen!**
tell it to the others

b) *combined with prepositions*

Some articles can be combined with a preceding preposition, for example an + das becomes ans. In some cases these combined forms are normal in both spoken and written German, in others the combined form is only used in spoken German:

| das | ans, ins |
|-----|----------|
| | *spoken German only:* aufs, durchs, fürs, hinters, übers, ums, unters, vors |
| | **sie ging ans Fenster** |
| | she went to the window |
| | **es geht ums Überleben** |
| | it's a question of survival |
| dem | am, beim, im, vom, zum |
| | *spoken German only:* hinterm, überm, unterm, vorm |
| | **ich gehe zum Bäcker** |
| | I'm going to the baker's |
| | **vorm Haus steht ein Baum** |
| | there's a tree in front of the house |
| der | zur |
| | **er fuhr zur Erholung in den Schwarzwald** |
| | he went to the Black Forest on a health cure |

The combined forms are sometimes not used if the writer or speaker wishes to emphasise the article:

**wo? – ach, in *dem* Wirtshaus**
where? – oh, in *that* pub

The combined forms are not normally used if the noun is followed by a relative clause (*see* pp 103-07):

**in dem Café, das gestern eröffnet wurde**
in the café that opened yesterday

## 2 Use

As in English, the definite article is used to indicate a specific person or thing:

**der Zirkus kommt**
the circus is coming

**die Disco hinter dem Rathaus**
the disco behind the town hall

Apart from cases where the usage is similar to English, the definite article is used:

a) *with the names of certain countries and geographical regions, especially ones that are feminine:*

| | | |
|---|---|---|
| **die Slowakei** | **die Türkei** | **die Schweiz** |
| Slovakia | Turkey | Switzerland |
| **das Elsass** | **der Sudan** | **der Balkan** |
| Alsace | the Sudan | the Balkans |
| **in der Türkei** | **wir fahren in die Schweiz** | |
| in Turkey | we're going to Switzerland | |

With some countries the article is optional:

| | | |
|---|---|---|
| **(der) Iran** | **(der) Irak** | **(der) Libanon** |
| Iran | Iraq | Lebanon |
| **im/in Iran** | | |
| in Iran | | |

Note that all geographical names have a definite article if they are preceded by an adjective:

**das alte Berlin**
old Berlin

except for the adjectives **ganz** and **halb**:

| | |
|---|---|
| **ganz/das ganze Schottland** | **halb/das halbe Europa** |
| the whole of Scotland | half of Europe |

b) *generally with abstract nouns:*

**für die Freiheit kämpfen**
to fight for freedom

**nichts geht über die Gesundheit**
nothing is more important than health

c) *with activities such as the arts, business, science, sports:*
**eine Sendung über die Botanik**
a programme about botany

**eine Einführung in das Bankwesen**
an introduction to banking

**die Entwicklung der Chemie**          **die moderne Leichtathletik**
the development of chemistry           modern athletics

Note that there is no article when such words are used for
school/university subjects:

**wir haben heute Chemie**          **Turnen ist mein Lieblingsfach**
we have chemistry today             P.E. is my favourite subject

d) *with* Mensch *when it refers to the species:*
**der Mensch ist ein Gewohnheitstier**
man is a creature of habit

e) *with the seasons, months, meals and times of the day:*

| | | |
|---|---|---|
| **am Abend** | **im Mai** | **zum Abendessen** |
| in the evening | in May | for dinner |
| **der Frühling kommt** | **in der Dämmerung** | |
| spring is coming | at twilight | |

---

## Note

• the article is not used when such words are combined with
adjectives to form adverb phrases. *Compare:*

**im Mai**
next May
*and*
**wir ziehen nächsten Mai um**
we're moving in May

• the article is not used after es ist/wird

**es ist schon Tag**                **es wird bald Winter**
it's day already                    it'll soon be winter

f) *as an alternative to* pro *to translate 'per':*

**150 Kilometer pro/die Stunde**
150 kilometres per hour

g) *with parts of the body and clothes where English would use the possessive:*

**heb die Hand!**
raise your hand!

**zieh ihm die Jacke aus!**
take his jacket off

**die Frau mit dem roten Haar**
the woman with red hair

h) *with types of transport, especially after prepositions:*

**mit dem Wagen**
by car

**mit dem Rad**
by bicycle

**auf dem Schiff**
on board ship

---

## Note

In many expressions composed of verb + preposition + noun the article used does not correspond to the English equivalent:

**zum Stehen kommen**
to come to a halt

**jemanden zur Vernunft bringen**
to make someone see reason

**aus der Mode sein**
to be out of fashion

Such expressions must be learnt as a whole.

---

**3** The definite article used as a pronoun

a) The definite article can be used as an alternative to the personal pronoun (*see* pp 87-91); this usage is most common in spoken German and usually occurs when the pronoun occupies the first position in the sentence:

**Paul Gruber? der ist mein Freund**
Paul Gruber? he's my friend

**Paul Gruber? den kenn' ich nicht**
Paul Gruber? I don't know him

b) The neuter article, **das**, is used as a demonstrative (translated by the English 'that') to refer back to people, things and whole sentences:

**die Frau? das ist meine Mutter**
that woman? that's my mother

**beeil dich! das ist der Zug**
hurry up, that's the train

**du fährst mit? das ist vernünftig**
you're coming? that's sensible

c) The definite article is used with the relative pronoun for the English construction 'the one/the person who':

**der, der es getan hat, soll sich melden**
the one who did it should own up

**gib es dem, der es am meisten braucht**
give it to the one who needs it most

d) When used as a pronoun, the definite article has separate genitive forms:

| MASCULINE | FEMININE | NEUTER | PLURAL ALL GENDERS |
|-----------|----------|--------|--------------------|
| dessen | deren | dessen | derer |

These forms are relatively uncommon. They are used in sentences of the type in (c) above:

**auf Kosten derer, die arbeitslos sind**
at the expense of those out of work

e) The genitive forms above are also used as an alternative to the possessives (**mein**=my *etc*) when the possessive itself might be ambiguous. The only difference is that the plural form is **deren** in these cases. This happens where there are two people to whom the possessive might refer back. Thus in the sentence

'she saw Fiona and her husband'

it is not clear whether it is Fiona's or the subject's husband that is being referred to. The **dessen** forms refer back to the last mentioned person. So, in:

**sie sah Petra und ihren Mann**

it is unclear whether she saw Petra's or her own husband, but in:

**sie sah Petra und deren Mann**

it is clear that she saw Petra and her – Petra's – husband.

 **B THE INDEFINITE ARTICLE**

## 1 Forms

The indefinite article in English has only one form: 'a' (or 'an').

In German the indefinite article changes its ending according to the gender and case of the noun after it. *For the use of the cases see* pp 51-3.

|     | MASCULINE | FEMININE | NEUTER |
|-----|-----------|----------|--------|
| *nom* | ein | eine | ein |
| *acc* | einen | eine | ein |
| *gen* | eines | einer | eines |
| *dat* | einem | einer | einem |

| **eine Frau** | **hier ist ein Stuhl** | **nimm einen Stuhl!** |
|---|---|---|
| a woman | here is a chair | take a chair |

| **die Mutter einer Schülerin** | **mit einem schweren Hammer** |
|---|---|
| the mother of a schoolgirl | with a heavy hammer |

## 2 Use

a) As in English, the indefinite article is used with nouns to indicate someone or something which is not precisely specified:

**hast du eine Zeitung gesehen?**
have you seen a newspaper?

ich möchte ein Bier
I would like a beer

b) Unlike English, German omits the indefinite article

(i) before the names of occupations or similar functions when they
have no adjective:

ich möchte Bäcker werden
I would like to be a baker

er ist Vegetarier
he is a vegetarian

sie ist Katholikin geworden
she has become a Catholic

*but:* **sie ist eine bekannte Pilotin**
she is a famous pilot

(ii) after als = as:

ich komme als Freund
I come as a friend

sie gilt als ausgezeichnete Ärztin
she is considered an excellent doctor

(iii) with names of nationalities used after the verb 'to be':

er ist Deutscher
he is a German

sie ist Französin von Geburt
she is a Frenchwoman by birth

## 3 The indefinite article used as a pronoun

a) *special forms*

When the indefinite article is used by itself as a pronoun, it has
the same forms as above, except that the masculine nominative
is einer and the neuter nominative and accusative is ein(e)s.

b) *use*

Used as a pronoun, it refers to some unspecified person or thing:

ein(e)s von den Mädchen
one of the girls

einer meiner Freunde
one of my friends

It is often an alternative to man:

**was soll einer da machen?**
what should one do?

> ## Note
>
> The accusative and dative forms are used for the accusative and dative of man:
>
> **man soll es offen sagen, wenn einem etwas nicht gefällt**
> you should say so openly if you don't like something
>
> **es kann einen schon ärgern, wenn man …**
> it can be very annoying if one …

## 4 irgendein

irgendein is usually translated by 'some … or other'. It has the same endings as ein and can be used both as an article and as a pronoun:

**irgendeiner hat's gesagt**          **irgendeine Ausrede**
someone or other said it              any old excuse

**wir werden irgendeinen Film sehen**
we'll see some film or other

For the plural, irgendwelche is used:

**hat jemand irgendwelche Fragen?**
has anyone any questions at all?

## 5 The indefinite article as adjective

ein can be used as an adjective after the definite article, a demonstrative or possessive. In such cases it has the appropriate adjective endings (*see* pp 64-72):

**der eine Besucher bleibt länger**
one of the visitors is staying longer

**die Frau des einen lebt noch**
the wife of one of them is still alive

 **C  kein (NO, NOT A, NOT ANY)**

kein has the same endings as the indefinite article ein, but also has
a plural form:

|  | MASCULINE | FEMININE | NEUTER | PLURAL ALL GENDERS |
|---|---|---|---|---|
| *nom* | kein | keine | kein | keine |
| *acc* | keinen | keine | kein | keine |
| *gen* | keines | keiner | keines | keiner |
| *dat* | keinem | keiner | keinem | keinen |

a)  It is used as a negative both for the indefinite article and for
    words without an article:

*positive*

**ich habe Zeit**
I have time

**ich habe einen Computer**
I have a computer

**ich habe Ferien**
I'm on holiday

*negative*

**sie hat keine Zeit**
she has no time

**er hat keinen Computer**
he hasn't got a computer

**er hat keine Ferien**
he's not on holiday

It is always used in cases where English uses 'not a':

**kein einziger Mensch kam**
not a single person came

b)  kein can also be used by itself, as a pronoun.

In that case, the masculine nominative singular is keiner, the
neuter singular nominative and accusative is kein(e)s:

**keiner weiß, wo er steckt**
no-one knows where he is

**D derjenige AND derselbe
(THE ONE; THE SAME)**

These are declined in two parts, the der part having the forms of
the definite article, the second part having regular endings for an
adjective after the definite article (*see* pp 64-6):

|  | MASCULINE | FEMININE | NEUTER | PLURAL ALL GENDERS |
|---|---|---|---|---|
| *nom* | derjenige | diejenige | dasjenige | diejenigen |
| *acc* | denjenigen | diejenige | dasjenige | diejenigen |
| *gen* | desjenigen | derjenigen | desjenigen | derjenigen |
| *dat* | demjenigen | derjenigen | demjenigen | denjenigen |

derselbe follows the same pattern.

a) derjenige can be used before a noun or by itself, as a pronoun.
   It is used to specify someone or something about which more
   precise information is going to be given. Thus it is always
   followed either by a relative clause or by a noun in the genitive
   or by a preposition + noun.

   A noun preceded by derjenige is always followed by a relative
   clause. derjenige tends to be avoided, especially in colloquial
   German.

   **diejenigen, die schon Karten haben, sollen vortreten**
   those who already have tickets should come forward

   **kennst du diejenigen Mitglieder, die dagegen gestimmt haben?**
   do you know the members who voted against?

b) derselbe is used both before a noun and by itself, as a pronoun.
   It is the equivalent to the English 'the same', except that it is
   written as one word:

   **das ist nicht mehr dieselbe Mannschaft**
   they're not the same team any more

   **es läuft auf dasselbe hinaus**
   it amounts to the same thing

> ## Note
>
> The article (der *etc*) in derselbe can combine with some
> prepositions. It is then written as two words:
>
> **im selben Haus**                    **zur selben Schule**
> in the same house                   to the same school
>
> **ins selbe Theater**
> to the same theatre

c) dergleichen *('suchlike, of that kind')*

   der gleiche is written as two words, except for dergleichen
   meaning 'suchlike'. dergleichen can be used before nouns or by
   itself, but in either case it does not change its form:

   **dergleichen Fälle**                 **nichts dergleichen**
   cases like this                      nothing of the sort

 **E DEMONSTRATIVES**

| dieser | jener | jeder | mancher | solcher | aller | welcher |
|--------|-------|-------------|----------------|---------|-------|---------|
| this | that | each, every | some, many a | such | all | which |

These are generally called demonstrative adjectives (or pronouns).
Adjectives that follow them have the same endings as after the
definite article.

**1** Forms

|     | MASCULINE | FEMININE | NEUTER | PLURAL ALL GENDERS |
|-----|-----------|----------|--------|--------------------|
| *nom* | dieser | diese | dieses | diese |
| *acc* | diesen | diese | dieses | diese |
| *gen* | dieses | dieser | dieses | dieser |
| *dat* | diesem | dieser | diesem | diesen |

The others have the same endings, except that jeder only occurs in the singular.

## 2 Use

a) dieser ('this')

Note that the neuter nominative and accusative is sometimes shortened to dies. dieser is used to point to a person or thing. It can be used before a noun or by itself, as a pronoun. It is very close to the English 'this':

**gefällt dir dieser Mantel?**
do you like this coat?

**nein, ich nehme diesen**
no, I'll take this one

It is often emphasised by the addition of hier or da after it or after the noun it goes with:

**diese Jacke hier ist schöner**
this jacket here is nicer

**aber probier diese da an**
but try on that one there

When standing alone before the verb sein (in all tenses) it is usually in the dies form, whatever the number or gender of the words it refers back to; the verb is singular or plural, according to the number of the noun following:

**dies sind meine Eltern**
these are my parents

**dies hier ist meine Tochter**
this is my daughter here

**dies(es) waren die besten Bilder**
these were the best pictures

b) jener ('that')

jener is relatively little used in colloquial German. The word for 'that' as opposed to 'this' is usually der/die/das (*see* c) below). In the following, somewhat formal, sentence, jene could be replaced by die, but is slightly more emphatic:

**er zeigte jene Kraft, die ihm zu vielen Siegen verholfen hatte**
he showed that strength which had brought him many victories

jener and dieser are used for 'the former' and 'the latter':

**Männer und Frauen, diese sorgen für andere, jene für sich**
men and women, the former care for themselves, the latter for others

c) **der, die, das**

The definite article is also used in German to mean 'that'.
Sometimes the word da is also added after the noun:

**der Mann (da)**                     **die Schule (da)**
that man                              that school

d) **jeder** *('each, every')*

jeder can be used before the noun or by itself, as a pronoun:

**jedes Kind weiß das**              **jeder soll kommen**
every child knows that               everyone's to come

The term jedermann is felt to be slightly stilted; jeder is the usual
German for 'everyone'.

jeder can be emphasised by the addition of ein before it; it still
has the same endings:

**ein jeder muss was mitbringen**
everyone has to bring something

e) **mancher** *('some, many a')*

mancher can be used before the noun or by itself, as a pronoun.
It indicates an uncertain number and translation can range from
'a few' to 'some', even 'many':

**manche älteren Leute**             **manche hundert Euro**
some older people                    a few hundred euros

**mancher Mann möchte reich sein**   **manches blieb unerledigt**
many a man would like to be rich     quite a lot of things were unfinished

i) In the singular manch can be used without endings before an
   adjective + noun:

   **sie hat manch schöne Stadt gesehen**
   she has seen many a fair city

This usage is highly literary.

ii) **manch** without endings can also be used before the indefinite article:

**manch eine interessante Geschichte**
many an interesting story

**manch ein Roman**
many a novel

Used without a noun the masculine nominative is **manch einer**:

**manch einer erfährt das zu spät**
many a man learns that too late

f) solcher *('such, such a')*

i) In the singular **solcher** is rarely used with particular persons or objects. It is normally used with names of qualities, abstract nouns or substances.

**solches Wetter!**
such weather

**mit solcher Geschwindigkeit, dass ...**
with such speed that ...

With particular persons or objects it is common to use **so ein**:

**so ein Fahrer**
a driver like that

**haben Sie so eine Schüssel?**
do you have a bowl like this?

ii) In the plural it can be used with all nouns:

**solche Frauen sind gefährlich**
such women are dangerous

iii) It can also be used by itself, as a pronoun, usually in the plural:

**ich kenne auch solche**
I know people/things like that, too

In the singular it is only commonly used without a noun when it is neuter, in the form **solches**:

**hast du je solches gehört?**
have you ever heard anything like it?

iv) **solch** can be used without endings before an adjective + noun:

**ein solch altes Schloss**
such an old castle

**solch schicke Möbel**
such smart furniture

v) solch without endings can also be used with the indefinite article:

**solch ein altes Schloss**　　　**mit solch einem Freund**
such an old castle　　　　　　　with such a friend

Used without a noun the masculine nominative is **solch einer**, the neuter nominative and accusative **solch eines**:

**solch einer war's**　　　　　**hast du je solch einen gesehen?**
it was one like that　　　　　　have you ever seen one like him?

vi) solcher can also be used after ein or kein. In that case it has the normal adjective endings (*see* pp 67-8).

*Compare:*
**bei solchem schrecklichem Sturm**
during such a terrible storm
*with:*
**bei einem solchen schrecklichen Sturm**

g) aller *('all, all the')*

i) In the singular aller can only be used together with nouns denoting qualities or substances or abstract nouns:

**bei aller Bewunderung**　　　**er hat alles Geld ausgegeben**
in spite of all my admiration　　he spent all the money

In the plural it can be used before any noun:

**alle Spieler**　　　　　　　**für alle Kunden**
all players　　　　　　　　　for all customers

**die beste von allen Gruppen**
the best of all groups

In the neuter singular and in the plural it can be used by itself, as a pronoun:

**alles in Ordnung?**　　　　**nach allem, was du mir gesagt hast**
everything all right?　　　　after all you've told me

**Sie müssen alle kommen**　　**alle waren dagegen**
you must all come　　　　　everyone was against it

## Note

- Note the common expressions:

  **alle Welt**                    **die ganze Welt**
  everybody                        the whole world

- with most masculine and neuter nouns in the genitive singular
  the normal form is allen:

  **allen Ernstes**
  in all seriousness

ii) Before an article, demonstrative or possessive the normal
   form is all, without any ending; the article, demonstrative or
   possessive retains its normal endings.

   Note that there is no German equivalent to 'of' in the English
   'all of':

   **all unsere Bekannten**
   all of our acquaintances, everyone we know

   **mit all diesem Geld**          **all die Männer**
   with all this money              all of the men

   As an alternative to all das and all dies, das alles and dies alles
   are possible.

   Word order: after a pronoun:

   | **es alles** | **mit uns allen** | **für sie alle** |
   |---|---|---|
   | all of it | with all of us | for all of them |

   *but:*
   before **beide** or a number:

   | **alle beide** | **von allen vier(en)** |
   |---|---|
   | both of them | of all four of them |

   There are two possible orders for this; 'all three came' can be
   translated by:

   **alle drei sind gekommen**
   *or*
   **sie sind alle drei gekommen**

h) welcher? *('which?')*

i) welcher is the interrogative article (sometimes called the interrogative adjective or pronoun). It can be used both before nouns and by itself, as a pronoun.

**welche Farbe nehmen wir?**
which colour shall we choose?

**bei welcher Familie wohnt sie?**
which family does she live with?

**welches gefällt dir am besten?**
which one do you like best?

**welche kommen mit?**
which of them are coming with us?

ii) Before the verb 'to be' (in any tense) the form welches is often used for all genders, singular and plural. The verb is singular or plural according to the number of the noun following:

**welches ist der nächste Weg?**
which is the shortest way?

**welches (welche) waren die besten?**
which were the best?

iii) welch may be used without endings before an adjective + noun to express an exclamation. This usage is rather literary, was für ein being generally preferred in colloquial German:

**welch furchtbarer Kampf!**
what a fearsome battle!

**was für ein schlechtes Spiel!**
what a poor game!

iv) welch can be used with the indefinite article before a noun to express an exclamation:

**welch ein schrecklicher Kerl!**
what an awful bloke!

v) welcher can also be used before a noun for exclamations; it is felt to be very stilted, although some standard phrases with feminine nouns are less so:

**welche Freude!**
what joy!

**welche Ehre!**
what an honour!

**welche Schande!**
what a disgrace!

vi) As an interrogative, welcher can introduce a clause which is the object of a verb of telling, showing *etc*; the verb in the welcher clause then goes to the end. welcher can be used in this way either before a noun or alone:

**sag mir, welche CD mehr kostet**
tell me which CD costs more

**weißt du, welche mehr kostet?**
do you know which one costs more?

vii) welcher can be used alone as an indefinite pronoun, replacing etwas, einige *etc*. In this usage it does not indicate a question. This is a very common colloquial usage:

**ich hab kein Geld mehr. Hast du welches?**
I've no money left. Have you any?

**lass sie zu Hause, ich habe welche**
leave them at home, I've got some

Note that the negative of welcher in this use is kein:

**bring sie mit, ich hab keine**
bring them with you, I haven't any

viii) welcher can be used as a relative pronoun without indicating a question. It is less common than der/die/das but is useful to avoid repetition:

**das ist die Bluse, welche sie gewählt hat**
that's the blouse she chose

**wähle die, welche dir gefallen**
choose the ones that you like

#  THE POSSESSIVE

## 1 Forms

There is a possessive form for each of the personal pronouns:

| PRONOUN | POSSESSIVE |
| --- | --- |
| ich | mein |
| du | dein |
| er | sein |

| sie | ihr |
|-----|-----|
| es | sein |
| wir | unser |
| ihr | euer |
| Sie | Ihr |
| sie | ihr |

They have the same endings as ein and kein, depending on the gender, number and case of the noun following:

|     | **MASCULINE** | **FEMININE** | **NEUTER** | **PLURAL** |
|-----|-----------|----------|--------|--------|
| *nom* | mein | meine | mein | meine |
| *acc* | meinen | meine | mein | meine |
| *gen* | meines | meiner | meines | meiner |
| *dat* | meinem | meiner | meinem | meinen |

with the same endings for dein, sein *etc*:

| **deine Tasche** | **mit unserer Hilfe** | **für Ihre Kinder** |
|------------------|-----------------------|---------------------|
| your bag | with our help | for your children |

## Note

- euer generally drops the -e- if it has an ending: eure, euren *etc*; unser often drops the -e- in spoken German, but it is normally kept when written.

- The possessives keep the same endings when they are preceded by aller, dieser, jener:

  **mit aller seiner Geschicklichkeit**   **diese meine Freunde**
  with all his skill                      my friends here

  *but:* **diese alten Freunde von mir**
  these old friends of mine

- For the replacement of the possessive by dessen or deren, *see* pp 20-1.

## 2 Use

a) The possessive can also be used by itself, as a pronoun; in such cases the masculine nominative has the form **meiner, deiner, seiner** *etc*, and the neuter nominative and accusative have the form **meines, deines, seines** *etc*. Colloquially **meines** *etc* is often shortened to **meins** *etc*:

**leih mir dein Rad, mein(e)s ist kaputt**
lend me your bike, mine is broken

**das ist ihr Platz, und das ist seiner**
that's her place and that's his

b) As an adjectival noun the possessive has some idiomatic usages:

**die Seinen**　　　　　　　　　**sie hat das Ihre getan**
his family　　　　　　　　　　she did her bit

**grüß die Deinen**
best wishes to your family

In sentences with noun + **sein** ('to be') + possessive, the possessives (except **Ihr/ihr**) often have no ending whatever the gender or number:

**der Pulli ist mein**　　　　　　**der Sieg war unser**
that sweater is mine　　　　　victory was ours

c) The possessive can be used with the definite article as a pronoun (alternative to a) above). In such cases it has the endings of an adjective after the definite article. This usage is generally regarded as literary:

**dieser Bleistift ist der meine**
this pencil is mine

**du hast kein Auto? fahr mit dem meinen**
you've no car? take mine

d) A further alternative is to use the form of the possessive plus -ig with the definite article: **der meinige, der deinige, der seinige, der ihrige, der unsrige, der eurige, der Ihrige, der ihrige.** This usage is also regarded as rather literary.

# 3 NOUNS

Nouns are naming words, which refer to persons, animals, things or abstract ideas. In German all nouns, not just proper names, are written beginning with a capital letter:

| **Haus** | **Ball** |
|---|---|
| house | ball |

## A GENDER

German nouns are either masculine, feminine or neuter in gender. The nouns themselves normally do not show this, but any preceding adjective or article 'agrees' with the noun by having the appropriate ending showing its gender plus number and case.

The gender should be learnt along with the noun, but often the meaning or ending will help you determine it, as set out in the guidelines below.

## 1 Masculine

**a)** *by meaning*

    i)   names of male humans and animals:

| **der Sohn** | **der Student** | **der Hahn** |
|---|---|---|
| son | student | cock |

          The name for the species may be masculine, feminine or neuter:

| **der Elefant** | **die Schlange** | **das Kamel** |
|---|---|---|
| elephant | snake | camel |

    ii)  names of days, months, seasons:

| **nächsten Mittwoch** | **letzten Mai** | **der Herbst** |
|---|---|---|
| next Wednesday | last May | autumn |

iii) points of the compass, winds, *etc*:

| der Süden | der Monsun | der Hagel |
|-----------|------------|-----------|
| south | monsoon | hail |

iv) makes of cars:

| ein BMW | ein Opel | ein Cadillac |
|---------|----------|--------------|

*but:*

motorcycles are feminine:

| die BMW | die Harley-Davidson |
|---------|---------------------|

v) names of rock and soil types:

| der Quarz | der Basalt | der Lehm |
|-----------|------------|----------|
| quartz | basalt | clay |

> *but:* **die Kreide**
> chalk

b) *by ending*

| -en | der Hafen | der Wagen |
|-----|-----------|-----------|
| | harbour | car |
| -er | der Arbeiter | der Kopfhörer |
| | worker | headphones |

> *but:*
> **das Fenster**  **das Messer**
> window  knife
> **die Mutter**  **die Tochter**
> mother  daughter

and a few other neuter and feminine nouns

| -ich | der Teppich | der Gänserich |
|------|-------------|---------------|
| | carpet | gander |
| -ig | der König | |
| | king | |
| -ismus | der Terrorismus | |
| | terrorism | |
| -ist | der Optimist | |
| | optimist | |
| -ling | der Frühling | mein Liebling |
| | spring | my darling |

| -or | **der Horror** | **der Motor** |
|---|---|---|
| | horror | motor |
| *consonant + s* | **der Schnaps** | **der Lachs** |
| | schnapps | salmon |

## 2 Feminine

a) *by meaning*

i) names for female humans and animals:

| **die Mutter** | **meine Frau** | **eine Kuh** |
|---|---|---|
| the mother | my wife | a cow |

ii) names for female occupations derived by adding -in to the masculine:

| **die Ärztin** | **die Journalistin** | **die Geologin** |
|---|---|---|
| doctor | journalist | geologist |

> ### Note
> Names of chemicals ending in -in are neuter:
>
> **das Benzin**
> petrol

iii) names of most common trees, fruits and flowers:

| | **die Pappel** | **die Kirsche** | **die Ananas** |
|---|---|---|---|
| | poplar | cherry | pineapple |
| | **die Kiefer** | **die Nelke** | **die Rose** |
| | pine | carnation | rose |
| *but:* | **der Ahorn** | **der Apfel** | **der Pfirsich** |
| | maple | apple | peach |

iv) makes of aeroplane and names of ships:

| | **die Boeing** | **die Graf Spee** |
|---|---|---|
| *but:* | **der Starfighter** | **der Airbus** |

v) numbers:

| **eine Null** | **die Sieben** |
|---|---|
| zero | (number) seven |

b) *by ending*

| | | |
|---|---|---|
| -a | **die Kamera** | **die Tuba** |
| | camera | tuba |
| -ei | **die Kartei** | |
| | card index | |
| *but:* | not compounds of **das Ei** (egg) | |
| | | |
| -enz | **die Frequenz** | |
| | frequency | |
| -heit | **die Freiheit** | |
| | freedom | |
| -ie | **die Chemie** | |
| | chemistry | |
| *but:* | **das Genie** | |
| | genius | |
| -ik | **die Technik** | |
| | technology | |
| *but:* | **der Atlantik** | **der Pazifik** |
| | Atlantic | Pacific |
| | **der Katholik** | |
| | Catholic | |
| -keit | **die Süßigkeit** | |
| | sweet | |
| -schaft | **die Mannschaft** | |
| | team | |
| -ung | **die Eroberung** | |
| | conquest | |
| *but:* | **der Schwung** | |
| | verve | |
| -tät | **die Pubertät** | |
| | puberty | |
| -tion | **die Reaktion** | |
| | reaction | |
| -ur | **die Natur** | |
| | nature | |

## **3** Neuter

a) *by meaning*

   i) names for the young of humans and animals:

   **das Kind**                    **das Baby**
   child                           baby

   **das Junge des Elefanten**
   the elephant calf

   Note that **das Junge** is an adjectival noun; *for endings see*
   section 4 *below*.

   **das Kalb**          **das Lamm**          **das Fohlen**
   calf                  lamb                  foal

   ii) names of continents, towns and most countries:

   **das Europa der 20er-Jahre**        **das Berlin meiner Kindheit**
   the Europe of the twenties           the Berlin of my childhood

   **das heutige Deutschland**
   modern-day Germany

   > *but:* names of countries always preceded by the definite article are
   > usually feminine or plural:
   >
   > **die Schweiz**        **die Türkei**        **die USA**
   > Switzerland            Turkey                the USA

   iii) most names for metals, chemical elements and drugs:

   **das Messing**        **das Uran**        **das Aspirin**
   brass                  uranium             aspirin

b) *by form*

   i) nouns formed from other parts of speech, especially infinitives:

   **das Vergnügen**        **sein Ja geben**        **das Hin und Her**
   pleasure                 to say yes               long deliberation

   ii) diminutives with the endings -chen, -lein:

   **das Mädchen**        **das Fräulein**        **das Städtchen**
   girl                   young woman             small town

iii) fractions (which take the suffix -tel):

**ein Sechstel**
a sixth

iv) collectives beginning with the prefix Ge-:

**das Gebirge**          **das Gerede**
the mountains           talk, gossip

c) *by ending*

| | | |
|---|---|---|
| -ing | **das Hearing** | **das Meeting** |
| -ma | **das Thema** | **das Dogma** |
| | subject | dogma |
| -ment | **das Regiment** | **das Appartement** |
| | regiment | flat |
| *but:* | **der Zement** | |
| | cement | |
| -tum | **das Eigentum** | |
| | property | |
| *but:* | **der Irrtum** | **der Reichtum** |
| | mistake | wealth |
| -um | **das Zentrum** | |
| | centre | |

## 4 Adjectival nouns

All adjectives – and many past participles – can be made into
nouns. As nouns, they begin with a capital letter but they keep the
adjective endings:

**der Deutsche**          *but*          **ein Deutscher**
the German                                a German

**viele Deutsche**        *but*          **alle Deutschen**
many Germans                             all Germans

*For the full list of endings see* pp 64–72.

# NOUNS

a) *masculine and feminine*

Masculine and feminine nouns formed from adjectives generally refer to people:

| **der Erste** | **die Letzte** | **ein Neuer** |
|---|---|---|
| the first one | the last one | a new one |

> ## Note
>
> When an adjective refers back to a noun there is no capital letter, the noun previously mentioned being understood:
>
> **zwei Läufer kommen, der deutsche führt knapp**
> there are two runners coming, the German is just in the lead
>
> *but*
>
> **der Deutsche hat gewonnen**
> the German won

b) *neuter*

Neuter nouns formed from adjectives most commonly refer to abstract ideas or qualities indicated by the adjective:

| **das Beste** | **das Erschreckende** |
|---|---|
| the best | what is frightening |

**das eben Gesagte**
what has just been said

   i) Such nouns are often used with an + dative:

      **das Interessante an dieser Geschichte**
      what is interesting about this story

      **das Schlimmste an der Sache**
      the worst thing about it

   ii) Such nouns are often used after etwas, nichts, viel, wenig, alles:

| **etwas Leckeres** | **nichts Neues** | **alles Gute** |
|---|---|---|
| something tasty | nothing new | all the best |

c) *names of colours*

Names for colours are formed from the adjective but there are forms both with and without the adjective ending.

i) The form without the adjective ending is usually the name for the general colour:

**das Blau des Himmels**          **Rot steht dir nicht**
the blue of the sky               red doesn't suit you

ii) The form with the adjective ending usually refers to some specific item of that colour:

**das Weiße seiner Augen**        **das Gelbe vom Ei**
the whites of his eyes            the yellow of the egg

---

Note

• For traffic lights the forms are Rot and Grün:

**bei Rot soll man halten, bei Grün darf man fahren**
you should stop on red, but at the green light you can go

• Note the plural for various shades of the same colour:

**die verschiedenen Rottöne des Gemäldes**
the different reds in the painting

---

## 5 Miscellaneous

a) The following words retain the same gender whatever sex of person they refer to:

| | |
|---|---|
| der Mensch | human being |
| der Gast | guest |
| die Geisel | hostage |
| die Person | person |
| die Wache | guard |
| die Waise | orphan |
| das Genie | genius |
| das Individuum | individual |

| | |
|---|---|
| das Staatsoberhaupt | head of state |
| das Opfer | victim |
| das Mitglied | member |

b) Compound nouns have the gender of the final component:

**die Urlaubsreise**
holiday trip

c) *For adjectival nouns see* **section 4** *above.*

d) Some nouns can have more than one gender:

| | | |
|---|---|---|
| **der Joghurt** | **das Joghurt** | **die Joghurt** *(colloquial)* |
| yoghurt | yoghurt | yoghurt |
| **der Teil** | **das Teil** | |
| part | part, component | |

Note that compounds with -teil have only one gender:

| | | |
|---|---|---|
| **der Vorteil** | *but* | **das Gegenteil** |
| advantage | | disadvantage |

e) The following are the most common nouns which change meaning according to gender:

Note that they usually have different plurals according to the gender.

| | MASCULINE (der) | FEMININE (die) | NEUTER (das) |
|---|---|---|---|
| Band | book, volume | band (*music*) | tape, tie |
| Erbe | heir | – | inheritance |
| Gehalt | content | – | salary |
| Golf | bay | – | golf |
| Heide | heathen | heath | – |
| Hundert | – | 100 (*number*) | 100 (*amount*) |
| Hut | hat | protection | – |
| Junge | boy | – | young animal |
| Kiefer | jaw | pine tree | – |
| Kunde | customer | news | – |
| Laster | lorry | – | vice |

| Leiter | leader | ladder | – |
| Mangel | lack | mangle | – |
| Maß | – | beer measure | measurement |
| Mensch | human | – | tart (*insult*) |
| Moment | moment (*time*) | – | moment (*physics*) |
| Otter | otter | viper | – |
| Pack | stack | – | rabble |
| Schild | shield | – | sign |
| See | lake | sea | – |
| Steuer | – | tax | steering wheel |
| Stift | pin, pencil | – | foundation |
| Tau | dew | – | rope |
| Tausend | – | 1000 (*number*) | 1000 (*amount*) |
| Tor | fool | – | gate, goal |
| Verdienst | income | – | merit |
| Weise | wise man | manner, tune | – |

##  THE FORMATION OF PLURALS

There are five main plural forms in German; three also sometimes have an umlaut on the stem vowel. These five forms are set out below with indications of the main types of nouns to which they apply. However, plural forms should be learnt together with the nouns.

### 1 No plural ending; some add an umlaut

Taken by: Masculine and neuter nouns ending in -chen, -el, -en, -er, -lein

| das Mädchen | die Mädchen | girl |
| der Hobel | die Hobel | plane (*carpentry*) |
| das Kabel | die Kabel | cable |
| der Braten | die Braten | roast |
| das Kissen | die Kissen | cushion |

| der Bagger | die Bagger | digger |
| das Messer | die Messer | knife |
| das Büchlein | die Büchlein | little book |

Some masculine and occasional feminine and neuter nouns take an umlaut:

| der Vogel | die Vögel | bird |
| der Laden | die Läden | shop |
| der Hammer | die Hämmer | hammer |
| das Kloster | die Klöster | monastery |
| die Mutter | die Mütter | mother |
| die Tochter | die Töchter | daughter |

## 2 Plural ending -e

Taken by: Most masculine nouns, many neuter nouns, a group of common feminine nouns of one syllable and the few feminines ending in -nis; the s is doubled after a -nis ending.

| der Tag | die Tage | day |
| der Freund | die Freunde | friend |
| der Dom | die Dome | cathedral |
| der Monat | die Monate | month |
| der Bericht | die Berichte | report |
| das Haar | die Haare | hair |
| das Pfund | die Pfunde | pound |
| das Gesetz | die Gesetze | law |
| das Ereignis | die Ereignisse | event |
| die Kenntnis | die Kenntnisse | knowledge |

All feminine monosyllables, many masculine monosyllables and some masculine words formed with prefix + monosyllable take an umlaut:

| die Hand | die Hände | hand |
| die Kunst | die Künste | art |
| der Traum | die Träume | dream |

| | | |
|---|---|---|
| der Knopf | die Knöpfe | button |
| der Einwand | die Einwände | objection |
| der Anfang | die Anfänge | beginning |
| *Note:* | das Floß | die Flöße | raft |

## 3 Plural ending -(e)n

> ### Note
>
> The e is included after words ending in -ei, -au, and consonants
> except for -el, -er endings; otherwise the ending is -n; the n is
> doubled after -in endings.

Taken by: A great many feminine nouns, a number of masculine
nouns, and a small number of neuter monosyllables. None take an
umlaut:

| | | |
|---|---|---|
| die Eitelkeit | die Eitelkeiten | vanity |
| die Hoffnung | die Hoffnungen | hope |
| die Ärztin | die Ärztinnen | doctor |
| die Bäckerei | die Bäckereien | bakery |
| die Au | die Auen | meadow |
| die Bahn | die Bahnen | railway |
| die Straße | die Straßen | street |
| die Schüssel | die Schüsseln | bowl |
| die Feder | die Federn | feather |
| der Mensch | die Menschen | human |
| der Nerv | die Nerven | nerve |
| das Bett | die Betten | bed |

## 4 Plural ending -er

Taken by: A good number of neuter nouns, especially
monosyllables, nouns ending in -tum, and a few masculine
monosyllables. All take an umlaut if possible:

| | | |
|---|---|---|
| das Rad | die Räder | wheel |
| das Land | die Länder | country |
| das Lied | die Lieder | song |
| das Gespenst | die Gespenster | ghost |
| das Bistum | die Bistümer | bishopric |
| der Reichtum | die Reichtümer | wealth |
| der Strauch | die Sträucher | bush |
| der Geist | die Geister | spirit |

## 5 Plural ending -s

Taken by: Many foreign nouns, especially from English and French,
nouns ending with a single vowel (except -e), abbreviations, proper
names, a few technical terms to do with the weather and the sea.
None take an umlaut:

| | | |
|---|---|---|
| das Team | die Teams | team |
| die City | die Citys | city centre |
| das Brikett | die Briketts | coal briquette |
| das Sofa | die Sofas | sofa |
| der Uhu | die Uhus | owl |
| ein Sozi | die Sozis | socialist |
| der Pulli | die Pullis | pullover |
| der Lkw | die Lkws | lorry |
| Frau/Herr Müller | die Müllers | the Müllers |
| das Tief | die Tiefs | depression (weather) |
| das Deck | die Decks | deck |

Note that all words deriving from English and ending in -y form
their plural with ys:

| | |
|---|---|
| das Baby | die Babys |

## 6 Double plurals

Some nouns have two plural forms which are different in meaning; those given below are the commonest:

| | | |
|---|---|---|
| die Bank | die Bänke | bench |
| | die Banken | bank |
| der Bau | die Baue | animal's lair |
| | die Bauten | building |
| die Mutter | die Mütter | mother |
| | die Muttern | nut (*for bolt*) |
| der Strauß | die Strauße | ostrich |
| | die Sträuße | bouquet |
| das Wort | die Wörter | single words |
| | die Worte | words (*in a sentence*) |

Note that the nouns with double gender listed on p 44-5 above will also have a different plural form for each gender.

## 7 Singular or plural?

Whilst almost all nouns have both singular and plural forms, some occur only in the singular and a few only in the plural. Usage here is not always the same as in English; consult a dictionary if in doubt.

a) *nouns only occurring in the singular:*

i) names of substances:

| | | |
|---|---|---|
| das Fleisch | das Gummi | die Milch |
| meat | rubber | milk |
| die Butter | das Leder | der Schnee |
| butter | leather | snow |

## Note

- These often form plurals by being compounded with either
  -sorten or -arten:

  **verschiedene Buttersorten**　　　　**zwei Getreidearten**
  different types of butter　　　　　　two kinds of grain

- Singular is sometimes used for plural:

  **zwei Bier, bitte**
  two beers, please

ii) many collectives:

| | | |
|---|---|---|
| **das Vieh** | **die Bourgeoisie** | **die Polizei** |
| cattle | the bourgeoisie | the police |
| **das Gepäck** | **der Schmuck** | **das Publikum** |
| luggage | jewellery | the audience |

iii) many abstract nouns:

| | | |
|---|---|---|
| **der Fleiß** | **die Hitze** | **der Aufbau** |
| diligence | heat | building up |

## Note

- Some abstract nouns can also be used in a specific as well as
  a general sense. In these cases they have a plural, eg der Spaß
  (enjoyment) has no plural, but der Spaß (joke) has the plural die
  Späße.

- Abstracts often have parallel forms which can be put into the
  plural, eg der Rat (advice) has no plural, but der Ratschlag (piece
  of advice) has the plural die Ratschläge.

iv) names of colours:

| | | |
|---|---|---|
| **das Schwarz** | **das Grün** | **das Blau** |
| black | green | blue |

Note that names for colours formed from the adjective with no ending can be used in the singular with plural meaning, eg **die zwei Grün** ('the two greens') (*see also* **section A4c**).

v) nouns formed from adjectives (*see* **section A4** *above*) when they do not refer to people and nouns formed from infinitives when they refer to an activity and not to an object:

**das Beste** ('the best thing') has no plural but **die Beste** ('the best woman') has the plural **die Besten**.

**das Schreiben** ('the act of writing') has no plural but **das Schreiben** ('the letter') has the plural **die Schreiben**.

b) *nouns only occurring in the plural:*

i) some geographical names:

**die Niederlande**
the Netherlands

ii) a few nouns of a collective nature:

| | | |
|---|---|---|
| **die Eltern** | **die Leute** | **die Ferien** |
| parents | people | holidays |
| **die Kosten** | **die Antiquitäten** | **die Möbel** |
| costs | antiques | furniture |

Note that modern German sometimes uses the awkward singular

**der Elternteil**
parent

 **C CASES**

There are four cases in German: nominative, accusative, genitive and dative. They are indicated by systems of endings (called declensions) on any articles or adjectives preceding the noun. There are also a few endings on nouns, as set out below.

The purpose of the cases is to indicate the relationship between nouns and other elements of the sentence or, alternatively, a noun's function in the sentence.

**1** The nominative

a) *as the subject of verbs:*

**der Mittelstürmer schießt**
*the centre forward* shoots

b) *after the verbs* **sein, werden, bleiben, heißen, sich betrachten als, sich nennen,** *and some other similar verbs where the noun complement to the verb is regarded as being in apposition to the subject:*

**er nennt sich mein Freund**
he calls himself *my friend*

**2** The accusative

a) *as the object of verbs:*
**der Schiedsrichter gab einen Elfmeter**
the referee gave *a penalty*

b) *after certain prepositions:* (see pp 201-13)

c) *in certain adverbial phrases, especially of time:*
**er sitzt den ganzen Tag herum**
he just sits around *all day*

d) *the so-called absolute accusative (literary usage):*
**den Mantel um die Schultern, ging er hinaus**
*his coat* over his shoulders, he went out

## 3 The genitive

a) *to express possession and similar relationships between two nouns:*

**das Büro seines Chefs**
*his boss's* office

**die Reparatur des Wagens**
the repair *of the car*

Note that this is very often used in contexts where the English genitive is also used.

b) *in certain adverbial phrases:*

**eines Tages**
one day

**meines Erachtens**
in my opinion

c) *after certain prepositions: (see pp 213-16)*

d) *when dependent on certain adjectives:*

**er ist sich seiner Verantwortung bewusst**
he is aware *of his responsibility*

## 4 The dative

a) *as the indirect object:*

**er gab seiner Frau den Brief**
he gave the letter *to his wife*

Note that by no means all German verbs that 'take the dative' are obvious from their English equivalents:

**er folgte dem Verbrecher**
he followed *the criminal*

b) *after certain prepositions: (see pp 196-200, 203-13, 215-6)*

c) *when dependent on certain adjectives:*

**sie ist ihrer Mutter sehr ähnlich**
she is very like *her mother*

##  D THE DECLENSION OF NOUNS

All masculine and neuter nouns end in -(e)s in the genitive singular.

Some masculine and neuter nouns, mostly monosyllables, can take an -e ending in the dative singular. This is optional and is normally used for reasons of rhythm. There are a few idiomatic expressions where it is required, eg im Grunde ('basically').

All nouns end in -n in the dative plural, except those forming the plural with -s.

### 1 Masculine

|     | SINGULAR | PLURAL |        |
|-----|----------|--------|--------|
| nom | der Vater | die Väter | father |
| acc | den Vater | die Väter | |
| gen | des Vaters | der Väter | |
| dat | dem Vater | den Vätern | |
| nom | der Tag | die Tage | day |
| acc | den Tag | die Tage | |
| gen | des Tag(e)s | der Tage | |
| dat | dem Tag(e) | den Tagen | |

a) A group of masculine nouns, often called weak nouns, takes the ending -(e)n in all cases apart from the nominative singular:

|     | SINGULAR | PLURAL |           |
|-----|----------|--------|-----------|
| nom | der Löwe | die Löwen | lion |
| acc | den Löwen | die Löwen | |
| gen | des Löwen | der Löwen | |
| dat | dem Löwen | den Löwen | |
| nom | der Christ | die Christen | Christian |
| acc | den Christen | die Christen | |
| gen | des Christen | der Christen | |
| dat | dem Christen | den Christen | |

| nom | der Student | die Studenten | student |
|-----|-------------|---------------|---------|
| acc | den Studenten | die Studenten | |
| gen | des Studenten | der Studenten | |
| dat | dem Studenten | den Studenten | |
| nom | der Herr | die Herren | gentleman |
| acc | den Herrn | die Herren | |
| gen | des Herr(e)n | der Herren | |
| dat | dem Herrn | den Herren | |

Masculine nouns which have -(e)n endings in the singular consist of:

i) nouns ending in -e denoting humans or animals:

| **der Erbe** | **der Zeuge** |
|--------------|---------------|
| heir | witness |
| **der Bulgare** | **der Biologe** |
| Bulgarian | biologist |

ii) a number of monosyllables ending with a consonant and denoting humans or animals:

| **der Bär** | **der Fürst** | **der Held** |
|-------------|---------------|--------------|
| bear | prince | hero |
| **der Mensch** | **der Narr** | **der Prinz** |
| human | fool | prince |
| **der Zar** | | |
| Tsar | | |
| *plus* | **der Bauer** | **der Nachbar** |
| | farmer | neighbour |

iii) words derived from foreign words with endings such as -ant, -ent, -graph, -ist and others; most, but not all, are names for human occupations:

| **der Emigrant** | **der Polizist** | **der Bürokrat** |
|------------------|------------------|------------------|
| emigré | policeman | bureaucrat |
| **der Astronom** | **der Automat** | **der Athlet** |
| astronomer | vending machine | athlete |

| | | |
|---|---|---|
| **der Doktorand** | **der Fotograf** | **der Pilot** |
| PhD candidate | photographer | pilot |
| **der Bandit** | | |
| bandit | | |

b) A small number of masculine nouns end in -(e)n in the plural and in the accusative and dative singular but form the genitive singular by adding -(e)ns; das Herz is similar except for the accusative singular:

| | SINGULAR | PLURAL | |
|---|---|---|---|
| *nom* | **der Name** | **die Namen** | name |
| *acc* | **den Namen** | **die Namen** | |
| *gen* | des Namens | der Namen | |
| *dat* | dem Namen | den Namen | |
| *nom* | **das Herz** | **die Herzen** | heart |
| *acc* | **das Herz** | **die Herzen** | |
| *gen* | des Herzens | der Herzen | |
| *dat* | dem Herzen | den Herzen | |

Similar to this is: **der Buchstabe** letter *(of alphabet)*

c) There is a small group of words with a double form in the nominative which take -ns in the genitive singular whichever nominative form is used:

| | |
|---|---|
| **der Friede/Frieden** | **der Funke/Funken** |
| peace | spark |
| **der Gedanke/Gedanken** | **der Glaube/Glauben** |
| thought | belief |
| **der Same/Samen** | **der Wille/Willen** |
| seed | will *(determination)* |

| | SINGULAR | PLURAL | |
|---|---|---|---|
| *nom* | **der Funke(n)** | **die Funken** | spark |
| *acc* | **den Funken** | **die Funken** | |
| *gen* | des Funkens | der Funken | |
| *dat* | dem Funken | den Funken | |

## 2 Feminine

|       | SINGULAR | PLURAL     |       |
|-------|----------|------------|-------|
| *nom* | die Frau | die Frauen | woman |
| *acc* | die Frau | die Frauen |       |
| *gen* | der Frau | der Frauen |       |
| *dat* | der Frau | den Frauen |       |

|       | SINGULAR  | PLURAL      |       |
|-------|-----------|-------------|-------|
| *nom* | die Nacht | die Nächte  | night |
| *acc* | die Nacht | die Nächte  |       |
| *gen* | der Nacht | der Nächte  |       |
| *dat* | der Nacht | den Nächten |       |

## 3 Neuter

|       | SINGULAR      | PLURAL       |          |
|-------|---------------|--------------|----------|
| *nom* | das Gebäude   | die Gebäude  | building |
| *acc* | das Gebäude   | die Gebäude  |          |
| *gen* | des Gebäudes  | der Gebäude  |          |
| *dat* | dem Gebäude   | den Gebäuden |          |

|       | SINGULAR    | PLURAL     |       |
|-------|-------------|------------|-------|
| *nom* | das Gras    | die Gräser | grass |
| *acc* | das Gras    | die Gräser |       |
| *gen* | des Grases  | der Gräser |       |
| *dat* | dem Gras(e) | den Gräsern |      |

## 4 Miscellaneous notes on forms

a) *-s or -es in genitive?*

 i) **-es** is always added after words ending in -s, -ß, -x, -z, -sch:

| der Krebs   | des Krebses   | der Sitz | des Sitzes |
|-------------|---------------|----------|------------|
| crab        |               | seat     |            |
| der Kitsch  | des Kitsches  |          |            |
| kitsch      |               |          |            |

 ii) **-es** is often added after a word which ends with a double consonant:

| der Kopf | des Kopfes | das Hemd | des Hemdes |
|----------|------------|----------|------------|
| head     |            | shirt    |            |

iii) -es is always added to

| Gott | Gottes |
|------|--------|
| God  |        |

iv) -s is normally added to words ending with an unstressed syllable:

| der Anfang | des Anfangs |
|------------|-------------|
| beginning  |             |

v) -s is normally added to words ending with a vowel or vowel + h:

| das Kino | des Kinos | der Schuh | des Schuhs |
|----------|-----------|-----------|------------|
| cinema   |           | shoe      |            |

vi) -s is added to most foreign nouns and to nouns of colour:

| das Restaurant | des Restaurants | das Rot | des Rots |
|----------------|-----------------|---------|----------|
| restaurant     |                 | red     |          |

vii) foreign words ending in -as, -os, -us have no extra ending in the genitive singular:

| der Mythos | des Mythos | der         | des         |
|------------|------------|-------------|-------------|
| myth       |            | Kommunismus | Kommunismus |
|            |            | communism   |             |

b) Neuter nouns ending in -nis double the -s before the genitive ending:

| das Bildnis | des Bildnisses |
|-------------|----------------|
| portrait    |                |

## 5 The Saxon Genitive

The so-called Saxon genitive in which the genitive word comes first is used for proper names (*see* section 6 *below*), eg Bachs Kantaten. Otherwise it is uncommon but is sometimes used in literary style:

**des Tages Hitze**
the heat of the day

## 6 The genitive of proper names and titles

a) All names take an -s ending in the genitive, whether masculine or feminine:

| Pauls Vater    | Monikas Freund   |
|----------------|------------------|
| Paul's father  | Monika's friend  |

i) Names consisting of more than one element take the -s on the last part:

**die Stücke Friedrich Dürrenmatts**
Friedrich Dürrenmatt's plays

Exceptions are some medieval names:

**die Werke Walthers von der Vogelweide**
Walther von der Vogelweide's works

ii) Names ending in -s, -ß, -x, -z cannot be dealt with in this way. The addition of -ens (eg Fritzens) was common but is now felt to be old-fashioned. The addition of an apostrophe after the -s is still sometimes used in written German (eg Grass' Stücke – 'Grass's plays'), but in general the problem is avoided by using von or des/der:

**der Einfluss von Marx**          **die Reise des Kolumbus**
Marx's influence                   Columbus's voyage

iii) The genitive -s is omitted when the proper name is preceded by an article in the genitive:

**die Zeugnisse der Luise**
Luise's school reports

b) When a name is preceded by a title, only the name takes the -s:

**die Politik Präsident Bushs**          **Tante Friedas Schmuck**
President Bush's policies                Aunt Frieda's jewellery
*but:* Herr is always declined (in the accusative and dative as well):
**Herrn Köpkes Angebot**          **Herrn Professor Winters Aufsatz**
Mr Köpke's offer                  Professor Winter's essay
**ein Brief an Herrn Doktor Schmidt**
a letter to Doctor Schmidt

Note that letters should be addressed to Herrn X; the word an is often put before, but is always understood anyway.

c) After statt, trotz, wegen neither title nor name is declined:

**trotz Peter**
in spite of Peter

**wegen Direktor Braun**
because of the director, Mr Braun

d) When preceded by an article, a demonstrative or possessive neither title nor name is now generally declined:

**das Schwert des General Herder**
General Herder's sword

e) Additional titles coming after the name are always declined:

**die Abdankung Eduards des Achten**
the abdication of Edward VIII

**das Leben Peters des Großen**
the life of Peter the Great

# 4 ADJECTIVES

Adjectives are describing words which usually accompany a noun (or a pronoun) and tell us what someone or something is like:

**ein kleines Dorf**
a little village
**meine Jacke ist blau**
my jacket is blue

**der neue Film**
the new film
**es war fantastisch**
it was fantastic

 **A AGREEMENT**

**1** Use

There is a major difference between English and German in the predicative use of adjectives (eg after 'is', 'are', 'were') and their attributive use (before nouns and pronouns). In the sentences

| PREDICATIVE | | ATTRIBUTIVE |
|---|---|---|
| my car is old | *and* | I drive an old car |

the word 'old' appears twice, in identical form. But in the German sentences

| | | |
|---|---|---|
| **mein Wagen ist alt** | *and* | **ich fahre einen alten Wagen** |
| my car is old | | I drive an old car |

the word **alt** appears once with and once without an ending.

The predicative use is so similar to English that it should not be a problem. However, German adjectives used attributively can prove troublesome, since only one of a number of endings is ever correct in a given context. The rules governing these endings are set out

below, but first here are some more examples to illustrate this
important difference:

| **PREDICATIVE** | **ATTRIBUTIVE** |
|---|---|
| **das Boot ist neu** | **ich brauche ein neues Boot** |
| the boat is new | I need a new boat |
| **seine Eltern waren reich** | **er kam mit seinen reichen Eltern nicht aus** |
| his parents were rich | he couldn't get on with his rich parents |

## 2 Endings

The endings of an attributive adjective in German are determined
by the noun which follows it, according to three factors:

a) its gender (whether masculine, feminine or neuter)

b) its number (is it singular or plural?)

c) its case (nominative, accusative *etc*)

In addition, there are variations, depending on whether the
adjectives comes after

a) a definite article (der, die, das *etc*)

b) an indefinite article (ein, eine *etc*)

*or*

c) is not preceded by any article, pronoun or possessive adjective.

## 3 Participles as adjectives

a) Present participles may be used as attributive adjectives:

**ein weinendes Baby**          **bellende Hunde**
a crying baby                     barking dogs

They can also be used in adjectival phrases:

**das gerade vorbeifahrende Auto**
the car that's just driving past

b) Past participles may be used both attributively (as an adjective and in a phrase) and predicatively:

| | |
|---|---|
| **die verlorene Stadt** | **das Geschirr ist abgewaschen** |
| the lost city | the dishes are washed |
| **die Reparatur der beschädigten Teile** | |
| the repair of the damaged parts | |

## 4 Exceptions

In some cases, the form of certain adjectives does not change, no matter what precedes them or what the gender, number or case of the following noun may be. These exceptions are:

a) *the adjective form of town names:*

**wer liest die Londoner Times?**
who reads the London Times?

**wir treffen uns in einem Glasgower Lokal**
we're meeting in a Glasgow pub

b) halb *and* ganz *with towns, countries and continents:*

| | |
|---|---|
| **in ganz Hamburg** | **ganz Schottland** |
| throughout Hamburg | the whole of Scotland |
| *but* | |
| **die ganze Schweiz** | |
| the whole of Switzerland | |

(*For the use of the article, see* **Articles A2**)

c) rosa, lila *and* prima:

| | |
|---|---|
| **ein rosa/lila Kleid** | **eine prima Idee** |
| a pink/lilac dress | a great idea |

Note that adjectives ending in -el and -er drop the e before the l or r when they are used attributively:

| | |
|---|---|
| **dunkel** | **ein dunkler Anzug** |
| dark | a dark suit |
| **teuer** | **eine teure Kamera** |
| expensive | an expensive camera |

## 5 Adjectives relating to countries

Adjectives formed from the names of countries or continents are written with an initial lower case letter, not a capital:

**italienisches Eis**
Italian ice-cream

**die französische Hauptstadt**
the French capital

## 6 Adjectives deriving from proper names

Adjectives formed from proper names ending in -(i)sch are now written with an initial lower case letter:

**das brechtsche Theater**
the Brechtian theatre

 ## B ADJECTIVE ENDINGS

## 1 After the definite article (der, die, das)

|  | MASCULINE | FEMININE | NEUTER | PLURAL ALL GENDERS |
|---|---|---|---|---|
| *nom* | -e | -e | -e | -en |
| *acc* | -en | -e | -e | -en |
| *gen* | -en | -en | -en | -en |
| *dat* | -en | -en | -en | -en |

Examples:

a) *nominative*

    *Masc Sing*

**der alte Mann wohnt hier**
the old man lives here

    *Fem Sing*

**die neue Rektorin heißt Ulrike**
the new headmistress is called Ulrike

*Neut Sing*

**das grüne Kleid ist besonders schick**
the green dress is extremely chic

*Plural*

**die blauen Fahrräder kosten mehr**
the blue bicycles cost more

**b)** *accusative*

*Masc Sing*

**haben Sie den alten Mann gesehen?**
have you seen the old man?

*Fem Sing*

**ich kenne die neue Rektorin schon**
I already know the new headmistress

*Neut Sing*

**niemand hat das grüne Kleid gekauft**
no-one has bought the green dress

*Plural*

**wo kann man die blauen Fahrräder bekommen?**
where can one get the blue bicycles?

**c)** *genitive*

*Masc Sing*

**das sind die Kinder des alten Mannes**
those are the old man's children

*Fem Sing*

**das Büro der neuen Rektorin ist rechts**
the new headmistress's office is on the right

*Neut Sing*

**der Preis des grünen Kleid(e)s ist zu hoch**
the price of the green dress is too high

*Plural*

**kennen Sie den Hersteller der blauen Fahrräder?**
do you know who manufactures the blue bicycles?

d) *dative*

*Masc Sing*

**die Nachbarn helfen dem alten Mann**
the neighbours help the old man

*Fem Sing*

**wir verstehen uns gut mit der neuen Rektorin**
we get on well with the new headmistress

*Neut Sing*

**im grünen Kleid sehen Sie gut aus**
you look good in the green dress

*Plural*

**mit den blauen Fahrrädern habe ich viel Erfolg**
I'm having a lot of success with the blue bicycles

Note that adjectives used after the following words take the same endings as for the definite article:

| | |
|---|---|
| **der/die/dasjenige** | the |
| **der/die/dasselbe** | the same |
| **dieser, diese, dieses** | this |
| **irgendwelcher** | some (or other) |
| **jeder, jede, jedes** | each |
| **jener, jene, jenes** | that |
| **mancher, manche, manches** | many a |
| **solcher, solche, solches** | such |
| **welcher?, welche?, welches?** | which? |
| **alle** *(pl)* | all |
| **beide** *(pl)* | both |

## 2 After the indefinite article

|       | MASCULINE | FEMININE | NEUTER |
|-------|-----------|----------|--------|
| *nom* | -er       | -e       | -es    |
| *acc* | -en       | -e       | -es    |
| *gen* | -en       | -en      | -en    |
| *dat* | -en       | -en      | -en    |

Examples:

a) *nominative:*

>   *Masc Sing*

>   **ein deutscher Film läuft heute im Kino**
>   there's a German film on today at the cinema

>   *Fem Sing*

>   **eine kleine Stadt liegt nicht weit von hier**
>   there's a little town not far from here

>   *Neut Sing*

>   **ein weißes Kaninchen wäre ein schönes Geschenk!**
>   a white rabbit would be a lovely present!

b) *accusative*

>   *Masc Sing*

>   **einen deutschen Film sieht man nicht oft**
>   you don't often get the chance to see a German film

>   *Fem Sing*

>   **das braucht eine halbe Stunde**
>   that will take half an hour

>   *Neut Sing*

>   **hast du ein neues Radio?**
>   have you got a new radio?

## ADJECTIVES

c) *genitive*

> *Masc Sing*

**der Titel eines deutschen Film(e)s**
the title of a German film

> *Fem Sing*

**im Laufe einer schlaflosen Nacht**
in the course of a sleepless night

> *Neut Sing*

**das Foto eines alten Schlosses**
the photo of an old castle

d) *dative*

> *Masc Sing*

**man unterhielt die Besucher mit einem deutschen Film**
the visitors were entertained with a German film

> *Fem Sing*

**nach einer langen Pause**
after a long pause

> *Neut Sing*

**außer einem langweiligen Fußballspiel war nichts los**
apart from a boring game of football there was nothing happening

> ## Note
>
> • In addition, adjectives used after the following words take the same endings as above, when used in the singular:
>
> | | |
> |---|---|
> | **irgendein/eine/ein** | **kein, keine, kein** |
> | some (or other) | no |
>
> also all possessive adjectives, eg **mein** (my), **Ihr** (your).
>
> • After **keine** and possessive adjectives in the plural, all adjectives end in **-en**, whatever case they are used in (*see* **section B1**).

**3** Without any preceding article

|  | MASCULINE | FEMININE | NEUTER | PLURAL ALL GENDERS |
|------|-----------|----------|--------|--------------------|
| *nom* | -er | -e | -es | -e |
| *acc* | -en | -e | -es | -e |
| *gen* | -en | -er | -en | -er |
| *dat* | -em | -er | -em | -en |

Examples:

a) *nominative*

>> *Masc Sing*

> **feiner Wein kostet viel**
> good wine costs a lot

>> *Fem Sing*

> **englische Studentin sucht Arbeit**
> female English student seeks work

>> *Neut Sing*

> **eiskaltes Wasser schmeckt gut**
> ice-cold water tastes good

>> *Plural*

> **junge Leute sind besonders willkommen**
> young people are especially welcome

b) *accusative*

>> *Masc Sing*

> **er hat furchtbaren Hunger**
> he is incredibly hungry

>> *Fem Sing*

> **Polizei fängt wilde Katze**
> Police catch wild cat

*Neut Sing*

**ich trinke gern eiskaltes Wasser**
I like drinking ice-cold water

*Plural*

**sie hat wunderbare Augen**
she's got wonderful eyes

c) *genitive*

*Masc Sing*

**ein Glas guten Wein(e)s genügt (more usual: guter Wein)**
one glass of good wine is sufficient

*Fem Sing*

**französischer Herkunft**
of French extraction

*Neut Sing*

**der Geschmack selbst gebackenen Brot(e)s**
the taste of home-made bread

*Plural*

**der Genuss alkoholischer Getränke**
the consumption of alcoholic drinks

d) *dative*

*Masc Sing*

**mit großem Erfolg**
with great success

*Fem Sing*

**aus guter Familie**
from a good home

*Neut Sing*

**unter lautem Stöhnen**
amid loud groans

*Plural*

**im Vergleich zu japanischen Managern**
in comparison with Japanese managers

Note the following points:

i) In addition, adjectives used after the following words take the
   same endings as above:

*singular only*

| | | |
|---|---|---|
| **ein bisschen** | **ein wenig** | **solch** |
| a little | a little | such |
| **viel** | **wenig** | **welch** |
| much | little | what! |

**solch würzigen Käse habe ich noch nie gegessen!**
I've never eaten such strong cheese!

**unter viel verdientem Beifall verließ sie die Bühne**
she left the stage to much deserved applause

*singular and plural*

| | | |
|---|---|---|
| **mehr** | **weniger** | **was für** |
| more | less, fewer | what (kind of) |

**mit mehr finanzieller Unterstützung**
with more financial support

**mit weniger regionalen Zeitungen**
with fewer regional newspapers

*plural only*

| | | |
|---|---|---|
| **einige** | **ein paar** | **einzelne** |
| some | some, a few | individual |
| **mehrere** | **viele** | **wenige** |
| several | many | few |

**es gibt nur noch ein paar schwierige Fälle**
there are just a few difficult cases left

**trotz mehrerer strenger Warnungen**
despite several stern warnings

*numbers*
**zwei drei vier** *etc*

**gegen den Rat zweier meiner Freunde**
against the advice of two of my friends

ii) After **etwas, mehr, nichts, viel** and **wenig**, but when used without
a following noun, adjectives are written with an initial capital
letter and take the same endings as a neuter noun (*see* p 42):

**nichts Besonderes ist heute passiert**
nothing in particular happened today

**wer hat (et)was Interessantes zu berichten?**
who has something interesting to report?

**er hat in seinem Leben nur wenig Gutes getan**
he hasn't done much good in his life

iii) If two adjectives come together before a noun, both take the
same endings:

**die Blätter des großen alten Baumes**
the leaves of the big old tree

**ein Kind mit gutem artigem Benehmen**
a well-behaved child

 ## C COMPARATIVES AND SUPERLATIVES

People or things can be compared to others by using:

**so** + **adjective** + **wie**
as + adjective + as

*or*

**ebenso/genauso/geradeso** + **adjective** + **wie**
just as + adjective + as

**er ist (eben)so groß wie ich**
he is (just) as tall as me/I am

However, when the comparison involves superiority the comparative
and superlative forms of the adjective are used.

Like in English, German adjectives form the comparative by adding -er and the superlative by adding -st or -est:

| **klein** | **kleiner** | **(der) kleinst(e)** |
|---|---|---|
| small | smaller | smallest |

This scheme is applied more consistently in German than in English:

| **intelligent** | **intelligenter** | **(der) intelligentest(e)** |
|---|---|---|
| intelligent | more intelligent | most intelligent |

## **1** Comparative adjectives

a) *formation*

i) As with adjectives in their basic form, comparative adjectives only take an ending (to indicate gender, number and case) when used attributively. These endings (*see* **section B**) are added to the standard -er of the comparative:

**die Farbe muss heller sein**
the colour must be lighter

*but:*

**wir möchten eine hellere Farbe**
we'd like a lighter colour

**dieses Nilpferd ist so dick!**
this hippo is so fat!

*but:*

**ein noch dickeres Nilpferd**
an even fatter hippo

Note that adjectives ending in -el and -er normally drop the e before the l or r when they are used in the comparative:

| **dieses Zimmer da ist dunkel** | **aber dieses hier ist dunkler** |
|---|---|
| that room is dark | but this one is darker |

ii) Some common one-syllable adjectives add an umlaut (and -er) in the comparative. The most common are:

| | | | |
|---|---|---|---|
| alt | (old) | älter | (older, elder) |
| arm | (poor) | ärmer | (poorer) |
| dumm | (stupid) | dümmer | (more stupid) |
| groß | (big, great) | größer | (bigger, greater) |
| hart | (hard) | härter | (harder) |
| jung | (young) | jünger | (younger) |
| kalt | (cold) | kälter | (colder) |
| klug | (clever) | klüger | (cleverer) |
| kurz | (short) | kürzer | (shorter) |
| lang | (long) | länger | (longer) |
| schwach | (weak) | schwächer | (weaker) |
| stark | (strong) | stärker | (stronger) |
| warm | (warm) | wärmer | (warmer) |

**ich brauche einen jüngeren Mann!**
I need a younger man/husband!

**mein Bericht war lang, aber deiner war bestimmt länger**
my report was long, but yours was definitely longer

iii) Note the comparative forms of the following:

| | | | |
|---|---|---|---|
| gut | (good) | besser | (better) |
| hoch | (high, tall) | höher | (higher, taller) |
| viel | (much, a lot of) | mehr | (more) |

b) *usage*

i) In addition to the attributive use of comparatives:
**ich kenne einen kürzeren Weg**
I know a shorter way

and the simple predicative use:

**Big Ben ist höher**
Big Ben is taller

an explicit comparison between two people or things can be made by adding **als**:

**sie bekommt ein höheres Stipendium als ich**
she gets a bigger grant than me/than I do

**ihre Bibliothek ist älter als unsere**
their library is older than ours

ii) Note, however, the set expression **denn je**:

**besser denn je**                    **weißer denn je**
better than ever                      whiter than ever

iii) Note, also, the construction **je** + comparative, **desto/umso** + comparative:

**je eher, desto besser**
the sooner, the better

**je heller die Farbe (ist), umso größer (ist) die Wirkung**
the lighter the colour (is), the greater the effect

iv) A small number of adjectives can be used in the comparative form without any obvious sense of comparison:

**eine ältere Dame**                  **auf längere Zeit**
an elderly lady                       for a while

## 2 Superlative adjectives

a) *formation*

i) The German superlative adjective is formed by combining the definite article (**der/die/das**) with an adjective plus suffix **-(e)st** and an ending.

ii) Superlatives take endings when used both attributively and predicatively. (Compare the basic form of adjectives and comparatives, which only take an ending when used attributively.)

iii) When used attributively, these endings, which are added to the **-(e)st** suffix, are the same as those in section B1:

**die berühmteste Philosophin ihrer Generation**
the most famous woman philosopher of her generation

**mit dem kostbarsten Ring der Welt**
with the most expensive ring in the world

Note that the **e** in adjectives ending in -el and -er is retained in the superlative:

**das dunkelste Zimmer von allen**
the darkest room of all

iv) The common one-syllable adjectives that add an umlaut in the comparative (*see* **section C1**) do the same in the superlative.

**der älteste Präsident der USA**
the oldest President of the USA

v) Note the following irregular forms of the superlative:

| gut  | (good)           | (der/die/das) best- *etc*   | (best)              |
|------|------------------|-----------------------------|---------------------|
| hoch | (high, tall)     | (der/die/das) höchst- *etc* | (highest, tallest)  |
| nah  | (near)           | (der/die/das) nächst- *etc* | (nearest, next)     |
| viel | (much, a lot of) | (der/die/das) meist- *etc*  | (most)              |

vi) Another form of the superlative adjective comes from combining **am** and an adjective plus -(e)sten:

**billig**          (cheap)          **am billigsten**          ([the] cheapest)

This construction can only be used predicatively or after the verb:

**dieser hier ist am billigsten**
this one here is the cheapest

Note that it does not have any endings.

b) *usage*

   i) Superlative expressions are often not complete without mention
      of the people or things which act as a reference group:

     **das schlechteste Wetter des Sommers**
     the worst weather of the summer

     **wer ist die mutigste von euch?**
     who's the bravest of you (girls/women)?

     The words **'des Sommers'** or **'von euch'** are the reference groups.

     If a reference group is mentioned, the form of the superlative
     adjective with the definite article is the one most commonly used.

   ii) If no reference group is mentioned, both the form with the
      definite article and that with **am** can be used:

     **diese Eier sind die billigsten/am billigsten**
     these eggs are (the) cheapest

     **er ist einfach der Beste**
     he's simply the best

   iii) A small number of adjectives can be used in the superlative
      form without any obvious sense of comparison:

     **es ist höchste Zeit**         **im äußersten Fall kostet es 2 Euro**
     it's high time             it'll cost 2 euros at the outside

   iv) To express 'in' as in phrases like 'the biggest in the world' *etc*,
      German uses either **in** or the genitive case:

     **die größte Stadt Deutschlands/in Deutschland**
     the biggest town in Germany

   v) Note also the following constructions with superlatives:

     **der meistgesungene Schlager**
     the most (frequently) sung hit

     **der meistgenannte Autor**
     the author mentioned most often

     as well as the set expression **bestgehasst** as in:

     **der bestgehasste Politiker**
     the most hated politician

# 5 ADVERBS

There are two main differences between German and English adverbs:

(a) many German adverbs have the same form as the corresponding adjective:

**die Wohnung ist billig** *(adj)*
the flat is cheap

**er lebt billig** *(adv)*
he lives cheaply

(b) the word order with adverbs often differs from English:

**sie übt oft Klavier**
she often practises the piano

**er fährt morgen nach Hause**
he's going home tomorrow

 **A FORMATION**

## 1 Words which are exclusively adverbs

da (there)
**da sind sie!**
there they are!

sehr (very)
**sehr nett**
very nice

geradeaus (straight on)
**nur geradeaus!**
keep straight on!

## 2 Adverbs identical in form with adjectives

| ADJECTIVE | ADVERB |
|---|---|
| schön (beautiful) | schön (beautifully) |
| furchtbar (terrible) | furchtbar (terribly) |

**sie ist schön, und sie singt auch schön**
she's beautiful, and she sings beautifully too

**er hat furchtbar gespielt – es war wirklich furchtbar, nicht?**
he played terribly – it was really terrible, wasn't it?

## 3 Adverbs formed from participles

| | |
|---|---|
| **sie spricht zögernd** | **übertrieben groß** |
| she speaks hesitantly | exaggeratedly large |

## 4 Adverbs formed from other parts of speech plus suffix

a) -lich

| ADJECTIVE | ADVERB |
|---|---|
| **neu** (new, recent) | **neulich** (recently) |
| **kurz** (short) | **kürzlich** (recently) |

**kürzlich bekamen sie einen Computer**
they recently got a computer

b) -mal(s)

| ADJECTIVE or NUMERAL | ADVERB |
|---|---|
| **jed-** (every) | **jedes Mal** (every time) |
| **manch-** (many a) | **manchmal** (sometimes) |
| **ein-** (one) | **einmal** (once) |
| **mehr-** (several) | **mehrmals** (several times) |

**er hat nur einmal geklopft**
he only knocked once

c) -ermaßen

| ADJECTIVE | ADVERB |
|---|---|
| **einig-** (some) | **einigermaßen** (somewhat) |
| **folgend-** (following) | **folgendermaßen** (as follows) |

**ich war einigermaßen überrascht**
I was somewhat surprised

d) -s

| NOUN | ADVERB |
|---|---|
| **(der) Mittag** (midday) | **mittags** (at midday) |
| **(der) Freitag** (Friday) | **freitags** (on Fridays) |

**mittags isst er in der Kantine**
at midday he eats in the canteen

e) -(er)weise

-weise can be added to the end of some nouns, -erweise to the end of some adjectives:

| NOUN or ADJECTIVE | ADVERB |
|---|---|
| **(der) Teil** (part) | **teilweise** (partly, in parts) |
| **begreiflich** (understandable) | **begreiflicherweise** (understandably) |

**Ihr Aufsatz ist nur teilweise gut**
your essay is only good in parts

**das ist normalerweise nicht der Fall**
that's not normally the case

## B USAGE

Adverbs are often used to qualify a verb, but as adverbial intensifiers they can also qualify adjectives and other adverbs.

**1** With a verb

**morgen schreibt er**                    **verlassen Sie uns hier?**
he'll write tomorrow                    are you leaving us here?

German usage makes a consistent distinction between position and movement in relation to adverbs. For native speakers of English the greatest difficulty is in translating 'here', 'there' and 'where?'.

| | | |
|---|---|---|
| **wir wohnen hier** | *but:* | **sie fährt hierher** |
| we live here | | she's driving here (= to here) |
| **sie saß da/dort** | *but:* | **er lief dahin/dorthin** |
| she was sitting there | | he ran there (= to there) |
| **wo arbeiten Sie?** | *but:* | **wohin fliegen Sie?** |
| where do you work? | | where are you flying (to)? |
| **wo wartet er?** | *but:* | **woher kommt er?** |
| where is he waiting? | | where does he come from? |

Note that in conversation the suffixes -hin and -her often go to the end of the clause:

**da gehen wir nie hin!**
we never go there!

**wo kommen Sie her?**
where do you come from?

## 2 With an adjective

**das ist fast einmalig**
that's almost unique
**es war unglaublich kalt**
it was unbelievably cold

**ein sehr langweiliges Buch**
a very boring book

## 3 With another adverb

**ich koche ebenso gut**
I cook just as well
**er schreibt erstaunlich schnell**
he writes amazingly quickly

**atme schön tief!**
breathe nice and deeply!

 **WORD ORDER**

## 1 Qualifying an adjective or another adverb

Adverbs come immediately before the adjective or adverb they qualify:

**sehr gut**
very good/well
**immer länger**
longer and longer
**viel lieber**
much rather

**ganz hoch**
quite tall/high
**äußerst dünn**
extremely thin(ly)
**weiter rechts**
further (along) on the right

*but:* **gut genug**
good enough

## 2 Qualifying a verb

a) In statements the normal position of the adverb is at the end
of the clause, but before a past participle, infinitive, separable
prefix and, in a subordinate clause, before the finite verb:

**Herr Braun liest nicht oft**       **sie hat neulich geschrieben**
Mr Braun doesn't read much     she wrote recently
**ich weiß, dass er das Geschenk morgen bringt**
I know he'll bring the present tomorrow

Note that adverbs of time often occur before a noun in the
accusative case:

**wir haben heute unsere Weihnachtskarten geschrieben**
we've written our Christmas cards today

b) In direct questions the order of the subject and finite verb
is reversed, but the normal position of the adverb otherwise
remains as in a):

**liest Herr Braun nicht oft?**     **hat sie neulich geschrieben?**
doesn't Mr Braun often read?    has she written recently?

In indirect questions the position of an adverb in the
subordinate clause is as in a):

**er hat gefragt, ob sie neulich geschrieben hat**
he asked if she had written recently

c) In a simple command the normal position of the adverb is after
Sie and wir, or after the finite verb (in the case of the du and ihr
forms of the imperative):

**bleiben Sie da!**       **gehen wir morgen baden!**
stay there!      let's go swimming tomorrow!
**fahr langsamer!**     **esst schnell euer Frühstück!**
drive more slowly!    eat your breakfast quickly!

**3** Sequence of Adverbs

a) When two or more adverbs (or adverbial phrases) appear in the same sentence, they usually do so in the following sequence:

1) TIME
2) MANNER
3) PLACE

**ich bleibe oft alleine zu Hause**
I often stay at home by myself

**wer fährt diesen Sommer per Anhalter ins Ausland?**
who's going hitching abroad this summer?

**joggen wir jetzt schnell durch den Park**
let's jog quickly through the park now

If a cause or reason is included it usually occurs after an expression of time:

**er ist gestern Abend wegen der Kälte früh ins Bett gegangen**
he went to bed early last night because of the cold

Note that with two expressions of time, the more general one comes first:

**sie kommen morgen um 5 Uhr an**
they're arriving at 5 o'clock tomorrow

b) If several adverbial items are used, it is common for one to be placed at the beginning of the sentence. This may be for special emphasis or for stylistic reasons, since a long string of items can be cumbersome.

*Compare:*

**letzten Montag hat sie ihn aus Eifersucht mit einem Hammer in ihrem Schlafzimmer getötet**
last Monday she killed him out of jealousy with a hammer in her bedroom

*with*

**aus Eifersucht hat sie ihn letzten Montag mit einem Hammer in ihrem Schlafzimmer getötet**
it was out of jealousy that she killed him last Monday with a hammer in her bedroom

*and*

**mit einem Hammer hat sie ihn letzten Montag aus Eifersucht in ihrem Schlafzimmer getötet**

*and*

**in ihrem Schlafzimmer hat sie ihn letzten Montag aus Eifersucht mit einem Hammer getötet**

# D COMPARATIVES AND SUPERLATIVES

## 1 Comparative adverbs

a) Comparative adverbs, like comparative adjectives, are formed by adding -er to the standard form. This only applies to adverbs with the same standard form as adjectives:

| ADVERB | COMPARATIVE ADVERB |
|---|---|
| **einfach** (simply) | **einfacher** (more simply) |
| **selten** (rarely) | **seltener** (more rarely) |
| **umstritten** (controversially) | **umstrittener** (more controversially) |

**könnten Sie das bitte etwas einfacher ausdrücken?**
could you put that a bit more simply, please?

**heutzutage kommt das seltener vor**
nowadays that happens more rarely

Note that the comparative form of gern is lieber:

**ich trinke gern Cola, aber ich trinke lieber Tee**
I like drinking coke, but I prefer to drink tea

*For other irregular forms see* Adjectives section C1.

**b)** 'than' is translated by **als**:

**er läuft schneller als sein Bruder**
he runs faster than his brother

**c)** **immer** + comparative renders the English double comparative:

**seine Stimme klingt immer unangenehmer**
his voice sounds more and more unpleasant

**sie bleibt immer länger von zu Hause weg**
she stays for longer and longer periods away from home

**d)** 'even' and 'all the' are translated by **noch** and **umso**:

**jetzt besuchen sie uns noch häufiger als im Vorjahr**
they now visit us even more frequently than last year

**nach einer Pause werden wir umso besser arbeiten können**
we'll be able to work all the better if we take a rest

## 2 Superlative adverbs

**a)** Superlative adverbs are formed by combining **am** with an adverb plus the ending **-(e)sten**. This only applies in the case of adverbs with the same standard form as adjectives:

| ADVERB | SUPERLATIVE ADVERB |
|---|---|
| **blöd** (stupidly) | **am blödsten** (most stupidly) |
| **selten** (rarely) | **am seltensten** (most rarely) |
| **elegant** (elegantly) | **am elegantesten** (most elegantly) |

**von allen hat sie sich am blödsten benommen**
she behaved most stupidly of all

**die Drossel kommt am seltensten**
the thrush comes the most rarely

Note that the superlative form of **gern** is **am liebsten**:

**ich reite gern, fahre aber am liebsten Rad**
I like riding, but like cycling best

b) When 'most' in English means 'very', rather than implying a comparison, it is usually translated by höchst, äußerst or sehr:

**höchst unwahrscheinlich**          **äußerst dankbar**
most unlikely                        most grateful

**das war sehr nett von Ihnen!**
that was most kind of you!

# 6 PRONOUNS

Pronouns are words which can substitute for nouns. They are divided into personal, reflexive, indefinite, relative and interrogative pronouns.

##  A PERSONAL PRONOUNS

### 1 Forms

|  | NOMINATIVE | ACCUSATIVE | GENITIVE | DATIVE |
|---|---|---|---|---|
| I | ich | mich | meiner | mir |
| you | du | dich | deiner | dir |
| he | er | ihn | seiner | ihm |
| she | sie | sie | ihrer | ihr |
| it | es | es | seiner | ihm |
| we | wir | uns | unser | uns |
| you | ihr | euch | euer | euch |
| you | Sie | Sie | Ihrer | Ihnen |
| they | sie | sie | ihrer | ihnen |

### 2 The translation of 'you'

du is used for the singular when talking to family, friends, children and animals; ihr is used for the plural. Sie is used when talking to people with whom you are not on 'du' terms. Nowadays young people often address each other by 'du' or 'ihr' even when they are not acquainted. A group containing a mixture of people you would call du and those you would call Sie can quite properly be addressed by ihr even though you would revert to Sie when talking to one individual. God and saints are addressed by du.

| | |
|---|---|
| **hast du die Hausaufgaben?** | **seid ihr schon zu Hause?** |
| have you got your homework? | are you home already? |
| **wie heißen Sie, bitte?** | **rechts sehen Sie das Schloss** |
| what is your name, please? | on the right you can see the castle |

## 3 The use of cases

a) *the nominative*

The nominative is used for the subjects of verbs and following the verb sein:

| | |
|---|---|
| **ich sehe** | **kannst du kommen?** |
| I see | can you come? |

| | | |
|---|---|---|
| **ich bin es** | **das sind wir** | **morgen gehen wir** |
| it's me | that's us | we're going tomorrow |

b) *the accusative*

The accusative is used for the direct object of verbs and after certain prepositions (*see also* pp 201–13)

| | | |
|---|---|---|
| **ich mag ihn** | **nimm uns mit!** | **ein Brief an dich** |
| I like him | take us too | a letter to you |

Note the use of an accusative object in wie ('such as') clauses where it is not used in English:

**das sind Berge, wie es sie in meiner Heimat gibt**
they are mountains such as we have at home

c) *the genitive*

The genitive form of pronouns is rare and is only used with a small number of verbs, prepositions (*see also* pp 213–16) and adjectives which are followed by the genitive:

| | |
|---|---|
| **er war ihrer satt** | **trotz seiner** |
| he was tired of her | in spite of him |
| **erinnerst du dich meiner?** | |
| do you remember me? | |

d) *the dative*

The dative is used for the indirect object of verbs and after certain prepositions (*see* pp 196-200, 203-13 *and* 215-6):

**ich gebe es dir**
I'm giving it to you
**nach Ihnen**
after you

**folgen Sie ihr!**
follow her
**bei uns**
at our house

## 4 Gender

Pronouns take the gender of the noun they replace. This means that English 'it' will often be translated by **er** or **sie**:

**wirf den Stuhl weg, er ist alt**
throw the chair away, it's old

**diese Tasche ist billig, kauf sie doch!**
that bag is cheap, go on, buy it

When a noun that refers to people does not have natural gender, there is no change in gender with the pronoun:

**und das Kind? – es kommt mit**
and the child? – he's/she's coming too

**er sah das Opfer, wie es weggetragen wurde**
he saw the victim being carried away

*but:*

**das Mädchen** may be referred to as either **es** or **sie**, the latter especially if grown up:

**das Mädchen, das dort tanzt, kennst du sie?**
do you know the girl who's dancing there?

Note the corresponding use of the possessive adjective **sein**:

**das Mädchen spielte mit seiner Puppe**
the girl was playing with her doll

## 5 Special uses of es

a) es can be used as an introductory subject when the noun which is the real subject comes after the verb. Whether the verb is singular or plural depends on the noun. This use sometimes corresponds to the English 'there was ...':

**es stand ein Mann vor dem Haus**
there was a man standing outside the house

**es tanzten viele Kinder**
a lot of children were dancing

When es is used in this way with sein it must be remembered that, unlike in English, the verb will be singular or plural depending on the noun following:

**es ist deine Freundin**          **es sind meine Eltern**
it's your girlfriend               it's my parents

Note that with a noun es comes before the verb, but with a pronoun the order must be pronoun + verb + es:

**ach, ihr seid's**                **ich bin es**
oh, it's you                       it's me

b) es is used as the object of sagen and tun where the English equivalent is 'so':

**du hast es gesagt**              **ich hoffe, es zu tun**
you said so                        I hope to do so

c) es is used after the verb sein to refer back to a noun or adjective in a preceding clause where in English the verb 'to be' stands alone:

**dieser soll besser sein; meinst du, dass er es ist?**
this one is supposed to be better; do you think it is?

d) Verbs which are followed by a dass clause or a zu + infinitive very often have an es as object, anticipating the clause or infinitive. There is no equivalent in English:

**ich liebe es, alte Filme zu sehen**
I love watching old films

**ich kann es nicht verstehen, dass er das vergessen hat**
I can't understand how he could have forgotten it

*See also the use of* es *for impersonal verbs* (pp 162-64).

# 6 The use of pronouns with prepositions

After most prepositions, the third person pronouns (er, sie, es) are usually only used to refer to people:

| | |
|---|---|
| **an sie** | **auf ihm** |
| to her | on him |

For a preposition + pronoun referring to an object or idea the form da(r)- + preposition is used:

| | |
|---|---|
| **damit** | **dagegen** |
| with it | against it |

There is an -r- when the preposition begins with a vowel: daran, darauf, daraus, darin *etc*:

**hast du es daraus genommen?**
did you take it out of here?

| | |
|---|---|
| **darin sind wir uns einig** | **ich erinnere mich daran** |
| on that we are agreed | I remember it |

This is the case with all prepositions except:

| | | |
|---|---|---|
| **außer** | **bis** | **gegenüber** |
| except | until | opposite |
| **ohne** | **seit** | **wider** |
| without | since | against |

and those taking the genitive:

| | | |
|---|---|---|
| **außerhalb** | **innerhalb** | **trotz** |
| outside | within | in spite of |
| **während** | **wegen** | |
| during | because of | |

and others less common.

*For the use of the definite article as an alternative to the personal pronouns see pp 19-21.*

**B REFLEXIVE PRONOUNS**

The reflexive pronouns are normally used in the accusative or
dative case. The forms are the same as the accusative and dative
of the personal pronouns except for the third person singular and
second person plural in the 'Sie' form:

| PERSON | ACCUSATIVE | DATIVE |
|--------|------------|--------|
| ich | mich | mir |
| du | dich | dir |
| er | sich | sich |
| sie | sich | sich |
| es | sich | sich |
| wir | uns | uns |
| ihr | euch | euch |
| Sie | sich | sich |
| sie | sich | sich |

Note that the reflexive is the only form of the pronoun where the
polite form does not begin with a capital letter.

There is a type of genitive which has the same forms as the genitive
of the personal pronouns. It is used with one or two adjectives,
usually together with **selbst**:

> **sie ist ihrer selbst nicht sicher**
> she's not very sure of herself

*For the use of the reflexive see* pp 165-67.

 **C INDEFINITE PRONOUNS**

Indefinite pronouns take the place of a noun but do not specify
precisely what they are referring to. Indefinite pronouns are, for
example, 'something', 'everyone'.

**1** man (one, you, people, they, we)

a) *forms*

| | |
|---|---|
| *nom* | man |
| *acc* | einen |
| *dat* | einem |
| There is no genitive form. | |
| reflexive | sich |
| possessive | sein |

b) *examples:*

**heute trägt man keine Hosenträger mehr**
people don't wear braces nowadays

**man sollte nie sagen, was einem gerade einfällt**
you should never say just whatever occurs to you

**im Büro hat man mir gesagt ...**
they told me in the office ...

**2** jemand (anyone, someone, somebody), niemand (no-one, nobody)

| | | |
|---|---|---|
| *nom* | jemand | niemand |
| *acc* | jemand(en) | niemand(en) |
| *gen* | jemandes | niemandes |
| *dat* | jemand(em) | niemand(em) |

The accusative and dative endings are often left out in spoken German and can be left out in written German.

| | |
|---|---|
| **hat jemand nach mir gefragt?** | **ich habe niemand(en) gesehen** |
| has anyone asked for me? | I saw nobody |

The reflexive form of both jemand and niemand is sich; the possessive adjective used with them is sein:

**niemand hatte sein Fahrrad dabei**
nobody had his/her bicycle with him/her
nobody had their bicycle with them

> **wenn jemand sich beschwert**
> if anyone complains

a) **jemand** and **niemand** can be combined with **sonst** (before them) or **anders** (after them) to mean 'someone/no-one else':

> **möchte sonst jemand es probieren?**
> would someone else like to try?

> **niemand anders als sein Bruder**
> none other than his brother

b) **jemand** can be made even less specific by the addition of **irgend**:

> **irgendjemand muss es verloren haben**
> someone or other must have lost it

> **komm mit irgendjemand**
> come with anyone at all

c) **jemand** and **niemand** can be combined with adjectival nouns for phrases of the type of 'somebody interesting' or 'somebody famous'. Although the adjective can have the -en ending in the accusative, the following is the commonest form:

| | |
|---|---|
| *nom* | jemand Interessantes |
| *acc* | jemand Interessantes |
| *dat* | jemand Interessantem |

Avoid the genitive by using **von jemand Interessantem**.

## 3 meinesgleichen (people like me, of my kind):

**meinesgleichen** does not change its form according to case:

> **sie redet nicht mit meinesgleichen**
> she doesn't talk to the likes of me

but forms are possible for all persons: deinesgleichen, seinesgleichen, unseresgleichen, euresgleichen, Ihresgleichen, ihresgleichen:

> **er redet nur mit seinesgleichen**
> he'll only talk to people on his own level

> **deinesgleichen kenne ich**
> I know your sort

> **ein Werk, das seinesgleichen sucht**
> a work in a class of its own

## 4 unsereiner (people of our sort, class)

unsereiner is singular; it can have accusative (unsereinen) and dative (unsereinem) and feminine forms (unsereine, unsereine, unsereiner):

> **unsereiner kann sich das nicht leisten**
> our sort can't afford that

> **unsereinem fehlt das Geld dazu**
> our sort haven't got the money for it

## D UNINFLECTED INDEFINITE PRONOUNS

There is a group of indefinite pronouns which remain the same whatever case they are in:

| etwas | nichts | jedermann |
|-------|--------|-----------|
| something | nothing | everyone |
| ein bisschen | ein paar | ein wenig |
| a little | a few | a little |

> **ich habe etwas/nichts gehört**
> I heard something/nothing

> **nichts war zu hören**
> nothing was to be heard

> **mit ein wenig Glück**
> with a bit of luck

With reflexive verbs they use the reflexive pronoun sich; jedermann uses the possessive sein, whereas beide and ein paar use ihr:

**nichts hat sich geändert**
nothing has changed

**jedermann hat seine Pflicht zu erfüllen**
everybody has his duty to do

**beide hatten ihre Hausaufgaben nicht gemacht**
neither of them had done their homework
both of them had failed to do their homework

## 1 etwas (something)

**es war etwas los**
something was going on

**hast du etwas gesehen?**
have you seen something?

etwas is shortened colloquially to was:

**ich werde dir was zeigen**
I'll show you something

etwas can be made even less specific by the addition of irgend:

**haben Sie irgendetwas gesehen?**
did you see anything at all?

**irgendwas muss geschehen sein**
something must have happened

etwas can be used as an adjective (it still has no endings) before nouns:

**etwas Brot**
some bread

**ich freue mich auf etwas Ruhe**
I'm looking forward to some peace and quiet

so etwas is used to mean 'something/anything like that':

**hast du je von so etwas gehört?**
have you ever heard of anything like it?

**so etwas musste kommen**
something like that was bound to happen

etwas is used with an + *dat* to translate 'something about':

**es ist etwas an ihm, was mir nicht gefällt**
there is something about him I don't like

etwas can be used with an adjectival noun for phrases of the type 'something remarkable' or 'something sad'. The adjective has the neuter endings of adjectives with no article (*see* pp 69-72):

**das war etwas durchaus Bemerkenswertes**
that was something quite remarkable

**die Erinnerung an etwas Trauriges**
the memory of something sad

**wir suchen nach etwas Besserem**
we're looking for something better

## **2** nichts (nothing, not anything)

**du hast nichts vergessen?**          **ich habe damit nichts zu tun**
you've not forgotten anything?        I have nothing to do with it

a)  nichts can be intensified by a number of words or phrases to make the equivalent of English 'nothing at all'. All the corresponding German words or phrases come before nichts:

**gar, ganz und gar, rein gar, überhaupt:**

**du hast überhaupt nichts getan!**
you've done nothing at all

**ich habe zu gar nichts Lust**
I don't feel like doing anything at all

b)  'nothing else, other than' is usually translated by sonst nichts:

**da war sonst nichts zu tun**
there was nothing else to do

c)  nichts ander(e)s als is usually the equivalent of 'nothing other than', though the English translation is often 'could only be described as':

**das ist nichts ander(e)s als Betrug**
that can only be described as fraud

d) nichts is used with an + *dat* for 'nothing about':

**nichts an der Sache gefällt dir**
you don't like anything about it

e) nichts can be used with an adjectival noun for phrases of the type 'nothing interesting' or 'nothing new'. The adjective has the endings of the neuter adjective without article (*see* pp 69-72):

**nichts Interessantes im Fernsehen?**
nothing interesting on TV?

## 3 ein bisschen (a little), ein paar (a few), ein wenig (a little)

These are all used without any change of form of either part. They can be used both by themselves as pronouns and before a noun:

**ein paar alte Bekannte**          **ein paar werden schon kommen**
a few old friends                    a few at least will come
**ich möchte ein bisschen frische Luft**
I'd like a bit of fresh air

## 4 jedermann (everyone)

jedermann takes a singular verb. It has no endings except for an **-s** in the genitive:

**jedermann hörte den Aufruf**
everyone heard the call

**das ist nicht jedermanns Sache**
that's not everyone's cup of tea

jeder is more common than jedermann; *see* p 28.

## 5 beide (both, the two)

**beide sind schon da**
both are here

a) **beide** can also be used after the definite article, a demonstrative
   or a possessive; in such cases it has the endings of an adjective
   after the definite article (*see* pp 64-6) whether it is used before a
   noun or by itself:

   **die beiden sind gekommen**
   the two of them have come

   **mit diesen beiden neuen Schülern**
   with these two new pupils

   Note the different word order to English:

   **die beiden Schüler**
   both the pupils

b) The singular **beides** is a neuter indefinite pronoun which can refer
   back to two objects or ideas but not to people. It is normally only
   used in the nominative (**beides**), accusative (**beides**) and dative
   (**beidem**):

   **Hut und Mantel, beides hat er vergessen**
   he's forgotten both his hat and coat

   **ich bin mit beidem zufrieden**          **beides ist teuer**
   I'm happy with either                      both are expensive

   **beides** is used with a singular verb except when sein is followed
   by a plural noun:

   **beides bietet Vorteile**               **beides ist richtig**
   both have advantages                      both are correct

   > *but:* **beides sind Erstaufführungen**
   > both are first performances

c) **beide** is only used in the plural and can refer to both people
   and objects:

| | |
|---|---|
| *nom* | beide |
| *acc* | beide |
| *gen* | beider |
| *dat* | beiden |

**beide wollen kommen**
both (of them) want to come

**beide waren gleich teuer**
both (of them) were just as expensive

d) *Word order:* **beide** can be used alone before the verb or come later in the sentence when a noun or pronoun is the subject:

| | |
|---|---|
| **beide wollen kommen** | **sie wollen beide kommen** |
| both want to come | they both want to come |
| **die Mädchen wollen beide kommen** | **leider kommen beide Mädchen** |
| the girls both want to come | unfortunately both girls are coming |
| **leider kommen die Mädchen beide** | |
| unfortunately both of the girls are coming | |

e) **beide** can be emphasised by having **alle** before it:

| | |
|---|---|
| **sind alle beide gekommen?** | **ihr seid Schurken, alle beide!** |
| have both of them come? | you're rascals, the two of you! |

f) **beide** after personal pronouns

The endings of **beide** can vary when it is used after personal pronouns. In general, **beide** has the same endings as plural adjectives without an article (*see* pp 69-72):

| | |
|---|---|
| **wir beide** | **für euch beide** |
| both of us | for the two of you |
| **sie beide zusammen** | |
| the two of them together | |

*except* after **ihr** and between **ihr** or **wir** and a noun:

| | |
|---|---|
| **ihr beiden** | **ihr beiden Freunde** |
| both of you | you two friends |
| **wir beiden alten Kumpel** | |
| we two old pals | |

Many other types of word can be used as indefinite pronouns:

*for the use as indefinite pronouns of the indefinite article, the possessives,* **derjenige, derselbe, dieser, jeder, keiner, mancher, welcher, alles, alle** *(plural) and* **solche** *(plural) see the individual entries in* Articles pp 25-33 *for the use of the interrogative pronoun* wer *as an indefinite pronoun see* p 107

*for* welcher *see* pp 32-3.

## E ADJECTIVES USED AS PRONOUNS

**1** A number of adjectives can be used without a following noun, ie as a pronoun. They generally have the normal adjective endings according to gender, number, case and whether they are preceded by an article or not:

**gestern war ein anderer da**
another person was there yesterday

**Folgendes muss getan werden**
the following must be done

It is often difficult to distinguish these from adjectival nouns.

**2** Some adjectives are most commonly used as indefinite pronouns in the plural.

a) einige ('some, several'), mehrere ('several'), viele ('much, many') and wenige ('little, few') are the most common:

| | |
|---|---|
| **ich habe einige schon bemerkt** | **der Beste unter vielen** |
| I've noticed several already | the best of many |
| **nur wenige sind erschienen** | **er kennt die Arbeiten mehrerer** |
| only a few turned up | he knows several people's work |

b) All (except mehrere) can also be used by themselves as pronouns in the singular, but with certain restrictions.

   i) einiges

   As a singular pronoun, einiges is only used as a neuter collective, not referring to people; its usual English equivalent is 'some things':

**einiges, was ihm neu war**
some things which were new to him

**ich habe einiges mitgebracht**
I've brought a few things with me

Like etwas and nichts, it can be used before adjectival nouns:

**einiges Interessante**
a few interesting things

ii) viel and wenig can have the neuter endings (vieles, vielem):

**wir haben viel(es) von ihm gehört**
we've heard a lot about him

**aus wenig(em) macht er viel(es)**     **nur wenig(es) gelang ihm**
he turns a little into a lot          not much turned out right for him

The forms with endings are more common in the dative:

**von vielem enttäuscht**
disappointed with many things

viel and wenig are very commonly used with adjectival nouns. The more common form is to use viel, wenig without endings whilst the adjectival noun takes the endings of a neuter adjective without an article:

**viel Überflüssiges**                **neben wenig Ausgezeichnetem**
much that is superfluous             alongside little that was excellent

**3** sämtlich ('all without exception') is generally used as a normal adjective but it can be used without an ending and following the verb to emphasise completeness:

**sie waren sämtlich erschienen**
they all came, every one

**F RELATIVE PRONOUNS**

The relative pronoun introduces a subordinate clause. It refers back to a preceding noun, pronoun or clause about which the relative clause provides further information or definition. For example, in the sentence, 'the man who did it', 'who' refers back to 'the man' and the clause 'who did it' tells us more about him.

As these are subordinate clauses, in German the verb goes at the end.

## 1 Forms

German generally uses the definite article for the relative pronoun.

|       | MASCULINE | FEMININE | NEUTER | PLURAL ALL GENDERS |
|-------|-----------|----------|--------|--------------------|
| *nom* | der       | die      | das    | die                |
| *acc* | den       | die      | das    | die                |
| *gen* | dessen    | deren    | dessen | deren              |
| *dat* | dem       | der      | dem    | denen              |

Note the change in form from the definite article for the genitive and for the dative plural.

**welche** is also used as a relative pronoun (*see* p 32-3).

## 2 Agreement

In English the relative pronouns 'which' and 'that' have only one form; 'who' has an accusative form 'whom' and a genitive 'whose'.

In German the form varies according to number, gender and case. The German relative pronoun takes its gender and number from what it refers back to, but takes its case from its function (subject, object *etc*) in the relative clause. For example, in the sentence:

**der Junge, den ich gestern sah**
the boy that I saw yesterday

**der Junge** is masculine singular; in the relative clause he is what was seen, ie the object; therefore the masculine singular accusative of the relative pronoun is used. *Compare also*:

**der Spieler, der gewonnen hat**
the player who won

**der Betrag, den du zahlen musst**
the amount you have to pay

**die Lehrer, denen er es erklären muss**
the teachers he has to explain it to

**die Frau, deren Mann du kennst**
the woman whose husband you know

**der Mann, dessen Frau du kennst**
the man whose wife you know

> ## Note
> The relative pronoun can never be omitted in German as it sometimes is in English:
>
> **die Frau, die du kennst**
> the woman you know

### 3 Use with prepositions

a) Prepositions always come before the relative pronoun, never at the end of the sentence as they sometimes do in English:

**die Hausaufgabe, von der du weißt**
the homework that you know about

**der Zug, mit dem er reist**
the train he'll be travelling on

b) When the relative pronoun used with a preposition doesn't refer back to a person but to an object or idea, then the form **wo(r)** +

preposition is frequently also used. *Compare*:

**die Ansagerin, von der er sprach**
the announcer he spoke about

*and:*

**das Thema, worüber er sprach**
**das Thema, über das er sprach**
the subject he spoke about

The form wor- is used with prepositions that begin with a vowel.

## 4 The alternative neuter form was

was is normally used for the neuter nominative and accusative to refer back to the following:

a) *indefinite neuter pronouns* such as alles, etwas, nichts (*for list see above*):

**nichts, was mich interessierte**
nothing that I was interested in

**etwas, was mir Sorgen machte**
something that worried me

**einiges, was ich bedenken sollte**
some things I should consider

When das is used instead of was, especially after etwas, it is because the speaker has something specific in mind. *Compare*:

**gibt es irgendetwas, was ich tun kann?**
is there anything I can do?

*and:*

**er sah etwas, das ihn schockierte**
he saw something that shocked him

b) *a neuter adjectival noun:*

**das Beste, was du tun kannst**
the best you can do

**das meiste, was ich gelesen habe**
the most that I have read

c) *a whole clause:*

**er sagte ab, was alle bedauerten**
he cancelled, which everyone regretted

**die Regierung trat zurück, was Neuwahlen erforderlich machte**
the government resigned, which led to a general election

Note that **was** is not used with a preposition:

**er rutschte aus, worüber alle lachten**
he slipped, which made everyone laugh

## 5 Replacement of the relative pronoun by wo (where)

a) Clauses of place are often introduced by the conjunction **wo** ('where') instead of the preposition + relative pronoun:

**ein Land, wo er viel Zeit verbrachte**
a country in which he spent a lot of time

b) When the relative refers back to the name of a country, town or place, **wo** must be used instead of a preposition + relative pronoun:

**Rom, wo es so viele schöne Kirchen gibt**
Rome, where there are so many fine churches

c) **wo** is also often used in place of a preposition + relative pronoun in clauses of time:

**die Jahre, wo er viel verdiente**
the years in which he earned a lot

**die Woche, wo ich verreist war**
the week in which I was away

## 6 wer as a relative pronoun

The interrogatives wer and was (*for forms see below*) can each be
used as relative pronouns without implying a question, when the
relative clause starts a sentence and is the subject of the main verb.
The English equivalent is usually 'anyone who' or 'whoever':

**wer das kauft, muss schwachsinnig sein**
whoever buys that must be daft

**wer wagt, gewinnt**
he who dares wins

**wem der Mut fehlt, darf gehen**
anyone who lacks the courage may go

## G INTERROGATIVE PRONOUNS

**1** There are two interrogative pronouns, one for persons
(wer) and one for things (was):

|  | PERSONAL | IMPERSONAL |
|-----|----------|------------|
| *nom* | wer | was |
| *acc* | wen | was |
| *gen* | wessen | wessen |
| *dat* | wem | - |

**wer kommt heute?**
who's coming today?

**was sagst du?**
what do you say?

**wessen Mantel ist das?**
whose coat is that?

**mit wem geht sie aus?**
who is she going out with?

**auf wen kann ich rechnen?**
who can I count on?

**2** They are all usually singular, but take a plural of the verb
sein if followed by a plural noun:

**wer sind deine Begleiter?**
who are your companions?

**was sind seine Gründe?**
what are his reasons?

**3** Use with prepositions

When used with a preposition, **was** is replaced by the **wo(r)** + preposition forms of the relative pronoun:

**womit soll ich es waschen?**
what shall I wash it with?

**woran liegt das?**
what's the cause of it?

**4** When the clause introduced by the interrogative pronoun follows a verb of saying, asking or similar, it is a subordinate clause (an indirect question) and the verb therefore goes to the end:

**weißt du, wer heute kommt?**
do you know who's coming today?

**erzähl mir, was er gesagt hat**
tell me what he said

*For the alternative use of* **welcher?** *as an interrogative pronoun see pp 32-3.*

## H THE ORDER OF PRONOUNS

*For a fuller treatment see pp 236-39.*

**1** Pronouns as direct and indirect objects generally come immediately after the verb:

**ich gebe dir das Geld**
I'll give you the money

**ich habe ihm das Buch geliehen**
I lent him the book

a) When there are two pronoun objects the accusative one comes before the dative:

**habe ich es dir gegeben?**
did I give it to you?

**ich habe es ihm geliehen**
I lent it to him

b) The same order applies when one is a dative reflexive pronoun:

**ich kann es mir nicht leisten**
I can't afford it

c) Otherwise the reflexive pronoun generally comes immediately after the verb:

**er kauft sich einen Filzstift**
he's buying a felt-tip pen

**2** A pronoun subject must come immediately after the verb when there is an inversion:

**morgens macht sie ihm das Frühstück**
in the mornings she makes his breakfast for him

**gestern hat sie ihn gesehen**
she saw him yesterday

**3** A noun subject can come before or after a pronoun object:

**gestern hat ihn meine Schwester gesehen**
**gestern hat meine Schwester ihn gesehen**
my sister saw him yesterday

# 7 VERBS

The section on verbs is divided into the following:

    A. Verb types and forms

    B. Notes on verb forms

    C. Use of tenses

    D. Conjugation tables

##  A VERB TYPES AND FORMS

### 1 Types of verbs

There are two main types of verb in German, generally referred to as weak and strong verbs. Weak verbs conform to a group pattern with a few standard variations. Strong verbs have a common basic pattern but a much greater degree of variation within it so that the main parts have to be learnt for each individual verb. There is a small number of verbs of mixed type. *For a list of the main parts of strong and mixed verbs, see* **pp 120-27** *and* **131-34**.

The fundamental difference between the two types is in the formation of the imperfect tense and the past participle: the weak verbs add a characteristic -t- to the verb stem (= infinitive without -(e)n ending) in these forms; strong verbs change the stem vowel of the infinitive when forming the imperfect tense and past participle, for example:

|         |         | IMPERFECT  | PAST PARTICIPLE |
|---------|---------|------------|-----------------|
| weak:   | packen  | ich packte | gepackt         |
| strong: | singen  | ich sang   | gesungen        |

These two basic types are similar to the two basic verb types in English (from the example above, English pack - packed - packed and sing - sang - sung). This similarity of verb form between English and German is very helpful in learning German verbs - but it does not always apply. However, if an English and German verb have the same root (eg packen - to pack, singen - to sing, sagen - to say, lieben - to love) the likelihood is that they will both be of the same type. Exceptions such as helfen (strong) and 'to help' (weak) should act as a warning to check if in doubt.

By far the largest number of verbs belong to the weak group. New creations are always weak (eg managen - gemanagt) and some verbs which were originally strong are gradually adopting weak forms (eg for the verb stecken ['to be in a situation'] in the imperfect tense the strong form stak is often replaced by the weak form steckte). Many strong verbs, however, are very common verbs, eg sein ('to be'), gehen ('to go') *etc.*

## 2 Tenses, moods and voices

a) *main tenses:*

   i)  present

  ii)  imperfect

 iii)  perfect

 iv)  pluperfect

  v)  future

 vi)  future perfect

b) *moods:*

   i)  indicative

  ii)  imperative

 iii)  subjunctive

 iv)  conditional

c) *voices:*

   i) active

   ii) passive

d) *the infinitive:*

The form in which the verb is usually given in dictionaries is called the infinitive. It consists of the verb stem plus (e)n. It is the equivalent of the English form with 'to': to read = **lesen** (les + en).

## 3 Verb forms: the conjugation of verbs

a) *weak verbs*

   i) Present tense

The present tense is formed by adding the endings -e, -st, -t, -en, -t, -en to the stem.

| *infinitive* | **fragen** | **reden** | **heizen** |
|---|---|---|---|
| ich | **frage** | **rede** | **heize** |
| du | **fragst** | **redest** | **heizt** |
| er/sie/es | **fragt** | **redet** | **heizt** |
| wir | **fragen** | **reden** | **heizen** |
| ihr | **fragt** | **redet** | **heizt** |
| Sie/sie | **fragen** | **reden** | **heizen** |

| *infinitive* | **atmen** | **klingeln** | **plaudern** |
|---|---|---|---|
| ich | **atme** | **klingle** | **plaud(e)re** |
| du | **atmest** | **kingelst** | **plauderst** |
| er/sie/es | **atmet** | **klingelt** | **plaudert** |
| wir | **atmen** | **klingeln** | **plaudern** |
| ihr | **atmet** | **klingelt** | **plaudert** |
| Sie/sie | **atmen** | **klingeln** | **plaudern** |

**haben** is a weak verb but has slightly irregular forms:

| ich | **habe** |
|---|---|
| du | **hast** |

| er/sie/es | hat |
|---|---|
| wir | haben |
| ihr | habt |
| Sie/sie | haben |

Standard variations:

An -e- is inserted before the -st and -t endings for verbs whose stem ends in -t or -d (*see* reden *above*). This is also the case with verbs whose stem ends in an -m or -n (but not -mm, -nn, -lm, -ln, -rm or -rn): *see* atmen *above*; filmen ('to film') would not need the extra -e-.

In verbs whose stem ends in -s, -ß, -x, -z the s of the -st ending is omitted (*see* heizen *above*).

Verbs whose infinitive ends in -eln lose the e before the l in the ich form (*see* klingeln *above*); this can also happen in verbs ending in -ern but is not obligatory (*see* plaudern *above*).

ii) Imperfect tense

The imperfect tense is formed by adding the endings -te, -test, -te, -ten, -tet, -ten to the stem.

| *infinitive* | fragen | reden | atmen |
|---|---|---|---|
| ich | fragte | redete | atmete |
| du | fragtest | redetest | atmetest |
| er/sie/es | fragte | redete | atmete |
| wir | fragten | redeten | atmeten |
| ihr | fragtet | redetet | atmetet |
| Sie/sie | fragten | redeten | atmeten |

haben loses the -b- of the stem in the imperfect tense:

| ich | hatte |
|---|---|
| du | hattest |
| er/sie/es | hatte |
| wir | hatten |
| ihr | hattet |
| Sie/sie | hatten |

Standard variations:

In verbs whose stems end in -d or -t, or in -m or -n (but not -mm, -nn, -lm, -ln, -rm or -rn): an e is inserted between the stem and the ending (*see* reden, atmen *above*).

iii) Perfect tense

The perfect tense is formed by using the past participle (*for the formation of the past participle see* section xiv *below*) with the present tense of sein or haben. *For the question of whether to use* sein *or* haben *see* pp 134–37 *below.*

| fragen | | reisen | |
|---|---|---|---|
| ich habe............... | gefragt | ich bin............... | gereist |
| du hast................. | gefragt | du bist............... | gereist |
| er/sie/es hat....... | gefragt | er/sie/es ist..... | gereist |
| wir haben............. | gefragt | wir sind............ | gereist |
| ihr habt................ | gefragt | ihr seid............ | gereist |
| Sie/sie haben..... | gefragt | Sie/sie sind...... | gereist |

The participle normally comes at the end of the sentence or clause.

iv) Pluperfect tense

The pluperfect is formed by using the past participle (*for the formation of the past participle see* section xiv *below*) together with the imperfect tense of sein or haben. *For the question of whether to use* sein *or* haben *see* pp 134–37 *below.*

| fragen | | reisen | |
|---|---|---|---|
| ich hatte............... | gefragt | ich war............... | gereist |
| du hattest............ | gefragt | du warst............ | gereist |
| er/sie/es hatte.... | gefragt | er/sie/es war... | gereist |
| wir hatten............ | gefragt | wir waren.......... | gereist |
| ihr hattet............. | gefragt | ihr wart............ | gereist |
| Sie/sie hatten..... | gefragt | Sie/sie waren.. | gereist |

The participle normally comes at the end of the sentence or clause.

v) Future tense

The future is formed by using the present tense of werden plus the infinitive:

fragen
ich werde............ fragen
du wirst................ fragen
er/sie/es wird.... fragen
wir werden......... fragen
ihr werdet........... fragen
Sie/sie werden.. fragen

The infinitive normally comes at the end of the sentence or clause.

vi) Future perfect

The future perfect is formed by using the present tense of werden plus the perfect infinitive (*see* **section xv** *below*). *For the question of whether to use* sein *or* haben *see* **pp 134-7** **below:**

| fragen | | reisen | |
|---|---|---|---|
| ich werde........... | gefragt haben | ich werde.......... | gereist sein |
| du wirst.............. | gefragt haben | du wirst............. | gereist sein |
| er/sie/es wird... | gefragt haben | er/sie/es wird.. | gereist sein |
| wir werden......... | gefragt haben | wir werden....... | gereist sein |
| ihr werdet.......... | gefragt haben | ihr werdet........ | gereist sein |
| Sie/sie werden. | gefragt haben | Sie/sie werden. | gereist sein |

vii) Imperative (*for usage and alternative forms see* **p 146** *below*).

There are imperatives for the du, ihr, Sie and wir forms of the verb. The imperative of the du form is the stem of the verb to which an -e is sometimes added; the others have the same endings as in the indicative. The du and ihr forms are normally used without a pronoun, the Sie and wir forms retain the pronoun but with inversion.

It is usual in German to have an exclamation mark at the end of an imperative.

| fragen | entschuldigen | klingeln |
|---|---|---|
| frag(e)! | entschuldige! | klingle! |
| fragen wir! | entschuldigen wir! | klingeln wir! |
| fragt! | entschuldigt! | klingelt! |
| fragen Sie! | entschuldigen Sie! | klingeln Sie! |

The -e- of the second person singular is normally left off, especially in spoken language; it is quite correct to omit it in written German. It is retained for verbs ending in -igen (*see* entschuldigen *above*).

Those verbs ending in -eln, -ern normally omit the e of the stem and retain the final -e (*see* klingeln *above*).

Verbs whose stems end in two different consonants retain the -e for reasons of ease of pronunciation (eg atme!, antworte!); verbs with a stem ending in -d or -t often keep the -e (red! or rede!, bet! or bete!).

viii) Present subjunctive

The present subjunctive is formed by adding the following endings to the verb stem: -e, -est, -e, -en, -et, -en.

| fragen | haben |
|---|---|
| ich frage | ich habe |
| du fragest | du habest |
| er/sie/es frage | er/sie/es habe |
| wir fragen | wir haben |
| ihr fraget | ihr habet |
| Sie/sie fragen | Sie/sie haben |

haben is regular in the present subjunctive.

ix) Imperfect subjunctive

The imperfect subjunctive for weak verbs is the same as the imperfect indicative (*see* section ii *above*).

haben has an umlaut in the imperfect subjunctive:

**ich hätte**
**du hättest**
**er/sie/es hätte**
**wir hätten**
**ihr hättet**
**Sie/sie hätten**

x) Perfect and pluperfect subjunctives

The perfect and pluperfect subjunctives are formed in the same way as the perfect and pluperfect tenses in the indicative except that the present or imperfect subjunctive of sein or haben is substituted for the present or imperfect indicative.

| fragen | | reisen | |
|---|---|---|---|
| ich habe/hätte.............. | gefragt | ich sei/wäre.................... | gereist |
| du habest/hättest......... | gefragt | du sei(e)st/wär(e)st......... | gereist |
| er/sie/es habe/hätte.... | gefragt | er/sie/es sei/wäre........... | gereist |
| wir haben/hätten.......... | gefragt | wir seien/wären.............. | gereist |
| ihr habet/hättet............ | gefragt | ihr seiet/wär(e)t.............. | gereist |
| Sie/sie haben/hätten.... | gefragt | Sie/sie seien/wären........ | gereist |

xi) Conditional: the subjunctive formed with würde

Very often the standard present, imperfect and perfect subjunctives are replaced by a compound form using the imperfect subjunctive of werden plus the infinitive or the perfect infinitive:

| fragen | |
|---|---|
| ich würde...................... | fragen |
| du würdest.................... | fragen |
| er/sie/es würde............ | fragen |
| wir würden................... | fragen |
| ihr würdet..................... | fragen |
| Sie/sie würden............. | fragen |

| | |
|---|---|
| ich würde...................... | gefragt haben |
| du würdest.................... | gefragt haben |

| er/sie/es würde............. | gefragt haben |
|---|---|
| wir würden..................... | gefragt haben |
| ihr würdet...................... | gefragt haben |
| Sie/sie würden.............. | gefragt haben |

xii) Passives

There are two forms of the passive in German, one using the auxiliary werden, the other using sein. Both use the past participle of the verb. F*or a distinction of the usage see* **pp 144-45** *below.*

| *passive with* werden | | *passive with* sein | |
|---|---|---|---|
| ich werde..................... | gefragt | ich bin...................... | gefragt |
| du wirst........................ | gefragt | du bist...................... | gefragt |
| er/sie/es wird................ | gefragt | er/sie/es ist.............. | gefragt |
| wir werden.................... | gefragt | wir sind.................... | gefragt |
| ihr werdet..................... | gefragt | ihr seid.................... | gefragt |
| Sie/sie werden.............. | gefragt | Sie/sie sind.............. | gefragt |

More complex tenses can be formed by using the other tenses of werden with the past participle:

*imperfect passive:*
ich wurde...              gefragt *etc*

*perfect passive:*
ich bin...                gefragt worden *etc*

Note the special form of the past participle of werden used to form the passive.

*pluperfect passive:*
ich war...                gefragt worden *etc*

*future passive:*
ich werde...              gefragt werden *etc*

*future perfect passive:*
ich werde...              gefragt worden sein *etc*

Passive subjunctives can also be formed by using the subjunctive of werden.

xiii) Present participle

The present participle is formed by adding -d to the infinitive. *For usage see* pp 155–56.

xiv) Past participle

The past participle is formed from the verb stem plus (e)t and normally begins with the prefix **ge-**:

| gefragt | geatmet | geheizt | geredet |

The final t is preceded by an e in verbs whose stems end in -d or -t or in a consonant preceded by a different consonant except for l or r.

In separable verbs the **ge-** is placed between the separable prefix and the verb stem, eg ausgefragt, zurückgereist, eingeatmet.

The prefix **ge-** is omitted in verbs with an inseparable prefix and verbs ending in -ieren:

| besucht | verletzt | übernachtet |
| erwartet | vollendet | telefoniert |

This also includes separable verbs ending in -ieren or those comprised of a separable prefix attached to a verb which already has an inseparable prefix:

**einstudiert**                    **anerkannt**

Verbs which can be separable or inseparable (*see* p 140) can have two past participles:

**übersetzt**   translated   **übergesetzt**   ferried over

xv) Infinitive

The infinitive is the basic form of the verb as it appears in dictionaries *etc.* It always ends in -(e)n and does not change its form, but different tenses of the infinitive can be created by combining it with auxiliary verbs:

| | |
|---|---|
| *infinitive* | **sehen** (to see) |
| *perfect infinitive* | **gesehen haben** (to have seen) |
| *passive infinitive* | **gesehen werden** (to be seen) |
| *passive infinitive* | **gesehen sein** (to be seen) |
| *perfect infinitive passive* | **gesehen worden sein** (to have been seen) |

**b)** *strong verbs*

i) Present tense

The present tense is formed by adding the endings -e, -(e)st, -(e)t, -en, -(e)t, -en to the verb stem. In some verbs the vowel of the stem changes in the second and third person singular.

| *infinitive* | **finden** | **sehen** | **fahren** |
|---|---|---|---|
| ich | **finde** | **sehe** | **fahre** |
| du | **findest** | **siehst** | **fährst** |
| er/sie/es | **findet** | **sieht** | **fährt** |
| wir | **finden** | **sehen** | **fahren** |
| ihr | **findet** | **seht** | **fahrt** |
| Sie/sie | **finden** | **sehen** | **fahren** |
| *infinitive* | **stoßen** | **gehen** | **werfen** |
| ich | **stoße** | **gehe** | **werfe** |
| du | **stößt** | **gehst** | **wirfst** |
| er/sie/es | **stößt** | **geht** | **wirft** |
| wir | **stoßen** | **gehen** | **werfen** |
| ihr | **stoßt** | **geht** | **werft** |
| Sie/sie | **stoßen** | **gehen** | **werfen** |
| *infinitive* | **sein** | **werden** | **bitten** |
| ich | **bin** | **werde** | **bitte** |
| du | **bist** | **wirst** | **bittest** |
| er/sie/es | **ist** | **wird** | **bittet** |
| wir | **sind** | **werden** | **bitten** |
| ihr | **seid** | **werdet** | **bittet** |
| Sie/sie | **sind** | **werden** | **bitten** |

Note that **sein** is completely irregular in the present tense.

The extra -e- is added to the du, er/sie/es and ihr forms for verbs whose stems end in -d or -t, except when there has been a vowel change. Compare **finden, bitten** above with:

| | | | | | |
|---|---|---|---|---|---|
| **laden** | **lädst** | **raten** | **rätst** | **schelten** | **schiltst** |
| **schmelzen** | **schmilzt** | **treten** | **trittst** | | |

The commonest changes of stem vowels in the du and er/sie/es forms are:

a → ä: *see* **fahren** *above*. Almost all strong verbs with a as a stem vowel modify it to ä, except **schaffen**; **backen** is nowadays commonly found without an umlaut and with a weak imperfect tense.

e (short) → i: *see* **werden, werfen** *above*. Most verbs with e (short) as a stem vowel modify it to i.

e (long) → ie: *see* **sehen** *above*. This is most common when e is followed by h:

| | | | |
|---|---|---|---|
| **befehlen** | **befiehlt** | **gebären** | **gebiert** |
| **geschehen** | **geschieht** | **lesen** | **liest** |

ii) Imperfect tense

Most strong verbs change the stem vowel for the imperfect tense; there is no ending added for the ich and er/sie/es forms; all the other forms have the same endings as the present tense.

| *infinitive* | pfeifen | finden | bleiben |
|---|---|---|---|
| ich | pfiff | fand | blieb |
| du | pfiffst | fandst | bliebst |
| er/sie/es | pfiff | fand | blieb |
| wir | pfiffen | fanden | blieben |
| ihr | pfifft | fandet | bliebt |
| Sie/sie | pfiffen | fanden | blieben |

| *infinitive* | schließen | helfen | sein |
|---|---|---|---|
| ich | schloss | half | war |
| du | schlossest | halfst | warst |
| er/sie/es | schloss | half | war |

| wir | schlossen | halfen | waren |
|---|---|---|---|
| ihr | schlosst | halft | wart |
| Sie/sie | schlossen | halfen | waren |

In the imperfect tense the -e- inserted after verb stems that end in -d, -t *etc* is felt to be particularly stilted. It is almost never inserted in spoken German and is normally avoided in written German except for the du forms of verbs whose stems end in -s, -sch, -x, -z (*see* schließen *above*) and for the ihr forms of verbs with stems ending in -d and -t (*see* finden *above*).

*For a list of strong verbs in the imperfect, see* **pp 173-78**.

Some verbs have a change in the final consonant of the stem, eg ziehen → ich zog. *See the list on* **pp 173-78**.

werden has an irregular imperfect tense as it changes the vowel but adds the weak endings (the older, strong form – ich ward, du ward(e)st, er ward in the singular – will occasionally be met in older literary works):

ich wurde
du wurdest
er/sie/es wurde
wir wurden
ihr wurdet
Sie/sie wurden

iii) Perfect tense

The perfect tense is formed by using the past participle (*for the formation of the past participle see* **section xiv**) with the present tense of sein or haben. *For the question of whether to use* sein *or* haben *see* **pp 134-37**:

| fahren | | | finden | | |
|---|---|---|---|---|---|
| ich bin............ | gefahren | | ich habe........... | gefunden | |
| du bist............ | gefahren | | du hast............ | gefunden | |
| er/sie/es ist... | gefahren | | er/sie/es hat... | gefunden | |

| | | | |
|---|---|---|---|
| wir sind............ | gefahren | wir haben......... | gefunden |
| ihr seid............. | gefahren | ihr habt............. | gefunden |
| Sie/sie sind...... | gefahren | Sie/sie haben... | gefunden |

The participle normally comes at the end of the sentence or clause.

iv) Pluperfect tense

The pluperfect tense is formed by using the past participle (*for the formation of the past participle see* **section xiv** *below*) with the imperfect tense of sein or haben. *For the question of whether to use* sein *or* haben *see* **pp 134-37** *below.*

| fahren | | finden | |
|---|---|---|---|
| ich war............. | gefahren | ich hatte............ | gefunden |
| du warst............ | gefahren | du hattest......... | gefunden |
| er/sie/es war... | gefahren | er/sie/es hatte. | gefunden |
| wir waren......... | gefahren | wir hatten......... | gefunden |
| ihr wart............. | gefahren | ihr hattet.......... | gefunden |
| Sie/sie waren.. | gefahren | Sie/sie hatten.. | gefunden |

The past participle normally comes at the end of the sentence or clause.

v) Future tense

The future tense is formed by using the infinitive with the present tense of werden:

| fahren | |
|---|---|
| ich werde.......... | fahren |
| du wirst............. | fahren |
| er/sie/es wird.. | fahren |
| wir werden....... | fahren |
| ihr werdet......... | fahren |
| Sie/sie werden. | fahren |

The infinitive normally comes at the end of the sentence or clause.

vi) Future perfect

The future perfect is formed by using the perfect infinitive (ie the past participle with the infinitive of **sein** or **haben**) with the present tense of **werden**. For the question of whether to use **sein** or **haben** *see* **pp 134–37.**

| fahren | | finden | |
|---|---|---|---|
| ich werde.......... | gefahren sein | ich werde.......... | gefunden haben |
| du wirst............. | gefahren sein | du wirst............. | gefunden haben |
| er/sie/es wird.. | gefahren sein | er/sie/es wird.. | gefunden haben |
| wir werden....... | gefahren sein | wir werden........ | gefunden haben |
| ihr werdet......... | gefahren sein | ihr werdet......... | gefunden haben |
| Sie/sie werden. | gefahren sein | Sie/sie werden. | gefunden haben |

vii) Imperative (*for usage and alternative forms see* **p 146**)

The imperative is used with the **du**, **ihr**, **Sie** and **wir** forms of the verb alone. The **du** form is the stem of the verb to which an -e is sometimes added; the others have the same endings as in the indicative. The **du** and **ihr** forms are normally used without a pronoun, the **Sie** and **wir** forms retain the pronoun but with inversion.

It is usual in German to have an exclamation mark at the end of an imperative.

**fahren**
**fahr(e)!**
**fahren wir!**
**fahrt!**
**fahren Sie!**

The -e ending of the **du** form is normally left off, especially in spoken German; it is quite correct to omit it in written German.

Verbs which change the stem vowel from **e** to **i** in the **du** form of the indicative also have the change in the imperative:

**sehen**
**sieh(e)!**

sehen wir!
seht!
sehen Sie!

*but:*

Verbs which change from a to ä do not have the change in the imperative (*see* fahren *above*).

Note that the du form of the imperative of werden is werde!

The imperative of sein:

sei!
seien wir!
seid!
seien Sie!

viii) Present subjunctive

The present subjunctive is formed by adding the following endings to the stem: -e, -est, -e, -en, -et, -en. No verbs change the stem vowel.

| *infinitive* | fahren | sehen |
|---|---|---|
| ich | fahre | sehe |
| du | fahrest | sehest |
| er/sie/es | fahre | sehe |
| wir | fahren | sehen |
| ihr | fahret | sehet |
| Sie/sie | fahren | sehen |

ix) Imperfect subjunctive

The imperfect subjunctive is formed by adding the endings -e, -est, -e, -en, -et, -en to the stem of the imperfect tense. If the vowel of the stem is a, o or u it always has an umlaut.

| fahren | bleiben | sein |
|---|---|---|
| ich führe | ich bliebe | ich wäre |
| du führest | du bliebest | du wär(e)st |
| er/sie/es führe | er/sie/es bliebe | er/sie/es wäre |
| wir führen | wir blieben | wir wären |
| ihr führet | ihr bliebet | ihr wär(e)t |
| Sie/sie führen | Sie/sie blieben | Sie/sie wären |

x) Perfect and pluperfect subjunctives

The perfect and pluperfect subjunctives are formed in the same way as the perfect and pluperfect indicatives (*see* **sections iii and iv** *above*) except that the present or imperfect subjunctive of **sein** or **haben** is substituted for the present or imperfect indicative.

| fahren | | finden | |
|---|---|---|---|
| ich sei/wäre.... | gefahren | ich habe/hätte.. | gefunden |
| du sei(e)st/ wär(e)st.......... | gefahren | du habest/ hättest............. | gefunden |
| er/sie/es sei/ wäre............... | gefahren | er/sie/es habe/ hätte................ | gefunden |
| wir seien/ wären.............. | gefahren | wir haben/ hätten............... | gefunden |
| ihr seiet/ wär(e)t............ | gefahren | ihr habet/ hättet............... | gefunden |
| Sie/sie seien/ wären.............. | gefahren | Sie/sie haben/ hätten.............. | gefunden |

xi) Conditionals or subjunctives with **würde**

As for weak verbs. *See* **section a) xi** *above*.

xii) Passives

As for weak verbs. *See* **section a) xii** *above*.

xiii) Present participle

As for weak verbs. *See* **section a) xiii** *above*.

xiv) Past participle

The past participle is formed from the verb stem (usually with a change of vowel) which is normally preceded by the prefix ge- and followed by -en:

| fahren | gefahren | bleiben | geblieben |
|---|---|---|---|
| werfen | geworfen | singen | gesungen |

The past participle of **sein** is **gewesen**

In separable verbs the ge- is placed between the prefix and the verb stem:

**einschlafen**     eingeschlafen     **aussteigen**     ausgestiegen

The ge- is omitted in verbs that have an inseparable prefix:

**verstehen**     verstanden     **empfehlen**     empfohlen

c) *modal verbs*

   i) Present tense

   The present tense has no endings on the verb stem in the ich and er/sie/es forms; the ending for du is -st, those for wir, ihr and Sie/sie are -en, -t, -en. The vowel of the verb stem in the singular is different from that of the infinitive and plural forms, except for sollen.

| *infinitive* | dürfen | können | mögen |
|---|---|---|---|
| ich | darf | kann | mag |
| du | darfst | kannst | magst |
| er/sie/es | darf | kann | mag |
| wir | dürfen | können | mögen |
| ihr | dürft | könnt | mögt |
| Sie/sie | dürfen | können | mögen |

| *infinitive* | müssen | sollen | wollen |
|---|---|---|---|
| ich | muss | soll | will |
| du | musst | sollst | willst |
| er/sie/es | muss | soll | will |
| wir | müssen | sollen | wollen |
| ihr | müsst | sollt | wollt |
| Sie/sie | müssen | sollen | wollen |

   ii) Imperfect tense

   The imperfect tense is formed with the same endings as weak verbs (*see* **pp 113-14**) but there is a change of stem vowel, except for sollen and wollen.

| *infinitive* | dürfen | können | mögen |
|---|---|---|---|
| ich | durfte | konnte | mochte |
| du | durftest | konntest | mochtest |
| er/sie/es | durfte | konnte | mochte |

| wir | durften | konnten | mochten |
| ihr | durftet | konntet | mochtet |
| Sie/sie | durften | konnten | mochten |
| *infinitive* | müssen | sollen | wollen |
| ich | musste | sollte | wollte |
| du | musstest | solltest | wolltest |
| er/sie/es | musste | sollte | wollte |
| wir | mussten | sollten | wollten |
| ihr | musstet | solltet | wolltet |
| Sie/sie | mussten | sollten | wollten |

Note the change of consonant in mögen.

iii) Perfect and pluperfect tenses

The perfect and pluperfect tenses are formed using haben. When the six modal verbs are used in their commonest function as auxiliary verbs the infinitive is used instead of the past participle:

| ich habe/hatte.............. | gehen dürfen |
| du hast/hattest.............. | gehen dürfen |
| er/sie/es hat/hatte...... | gehen dürfen |
| wir haben/hatten.......... | gehen dürfen |
| ihr habt/hattet.............. | gehen dürfen |
| Sie/sie haben/hatten... | gehen dürfen |

The modal verbs also have a regular past participle formed in the same way as those of weak verbs except that those that have an umlaut lose it:

gedurft    gekonnt    gemocht    gemusst    gesollt    gewollt

There is another form of the perfect tense using the present indicative of the modal verbs with the perfect infinitive of the verb, that is the past participle plus the infinitive of sein or haben:

| ich kann......... | gesehen haben | ich muss.......... | gefahren sein |
| du kannst....... | gesehen haben | du musst.......... | gefahren sein |

*etc*

For the distinction in sense between these two forms *see* pp 161–62.

iv) Future tense

The future tense is formed by the present tense of werden combined with the infinitive of the main verb and the infinitive of the modal verb:

ich werde............ kommen können
du wirst.............. kommen können
er/sie/es wird.... kommen können
wir werden......... kommen können
ihr werdet........... kommen können
Sie/sie werden... kommen können

v) Future Perfect

The future perfect is formed by the present tense of werden plus the perfect infinitive of the main verb and the infinitive of the modal verb. This clumsy form is almost never used. A sentence such as:

sie glaubt nicht, dass ich es bis morgen werde geschrieben haben können

is less common than the equivalent English form:

she doesn't think I will have been able to write it by tomorrow

The simpler form:

sie glaubt nicht, dass ich es bis morgen geschrieben habe

expresses practically the same idea.

vi) Present subjunctive

The present subjunctive is formed by adding the following endings to the infinitive stem: -e, -est, -e, -en, -et, -en.

ich könne
du könnest
er/sie/es könne
wir können
ihr könnet
Sie/sie können

vii) Imperfect subjunctive

The imperfect subjunctive is the same as the imperfect indicative, except that those modal verbs which have an umlaut on the stem vowel in the infinitive also have it in the imperfect subjunctive:

| ich | könnte | möchte | wollte |
|---|---|---|---|
| du | könntest | möchtest | wolltest |
| er/sie/es | könnte | möchte | wollte |
| wir | könnten | möchten | wollten |
| ihr | könntet | möchtet | wolltet |
| Sie/sie | könnten | möchten | wollten |

Note the change of consonant in mögen

viii) Perfect subjunctive

There are two forms of the perfect subjunctive.

One is formed with the present subjunctive of haben combined with the infinitive of the main verb and the infinitive of the modal verb:

ich habe............. sehen können
du habest........... sehen können
er/sie/es habe.. sehen können
wir haben........... sehen können
ihr habet............ sehen können
Sie/sie haben... sehen können

The other is formed by using the present subjunctive of the modal verb with the perfect infinitive of the main verb:

| ich könne.......... gesehen haben | ich müsse........... gefahren sein |
|---|---|
| du könnest........ gesehen haben | du müssest........ gefahren sein |
| er/sie/es gesehen haben könne............ | er/sie/es gefahren sein müsse............ |
| wir können........ gesehen haben | wir müssen........ gefahren sein |
| ihr könnet......... gesehen haben | ihr müsset.......... gefahren sein |
| Sie/sie können.. gesehen haben | Sie/sie müssen.. gefahren sein |

ix) Pluperfect subjunctive

There are two forms of the pluperfect subjunctive.

One is formed with the imperfect subjunctive of haben combined with the infinitive of the main verb and the infinitive of the modal verb:

ich hätte........... sehen können
du hättest......... sehen können
er/sie/es hätte. sehen können
wir hätten......... sehen können
ihr hättet.......... sehen können
Sie/sie hätten.. sehen können

The other is formed by using the imperfect subjunctive of the modal with the past infinitive of the main verb (*see* p 119-20):

| | | | |
|---|---|---|---|
| ich könnte........ | gesehen haben | ich müsste............. | gefahren sein |
| du könntest...... | gesehen haben | du müsstest.......... | gefahren sein |
| er/sie/es könnte............ | gesehen haben | er/sie/es müsste.. | gefahren sein |
| wir könnten...... | gesehen haben | wir müssten.......... | gefahren sein |
| ihr könntet........ | gesehen haben | ihr müsstet............ | gefahren sein |
| Sie/sie könnten.......... | gesehen haben | Sie/sie müssten.... | gefahren sein |

d) *verbs of mixed type*

i) A group of verbs has the endings of the weak conjugation but changes the stem vowel from -e- in the infinitive and present to -a- in the imperfect tense and past participle. Apart from this vowel change, they are perfectly regular weak verbs. They are: brennen, kennen, nennen, rennen:

| *infinitive* | *present* | *imperfect* | *past participle* |
|---|---|---|---|
| brennen | ich brenne | ich brannte | gebrannt |
| kennen | ich kenne | ich kannte | gekannt |
| *etc* | | | |

The imperfect subjunctive is also irregular:

| | |
|---|---|
| ich brennte | ich kennte |

*etc*

ii) Two verbs which can conjugate in this way can also have a regular weak imperfect and past participle:

| *infinitive* | *present* | *imperfect* | *past participle* |
|---|---|---|---|
| senden | ich sende | ich sandte | gesandt |
| | *etc* | ich sendete | gesendet |
| wenden | ich wende | ich wandte | gewandt |
| | *etc* | ich wendete | gewendet |

They have only one imperfect subjunctive form which is the same as the regular weak imperfect indicative.

Note the difference in meaning for **senden**:

| **senden** | (regular weak verb) | = to broadcast |
|---|---|---|
| | (mixed verb) | = to send |

Both forms can be used for most meanings of **wenden**; the form with the vowel change being slightly more literary. **wenden** meaning 'to turn' in sewing must have the regular forms.

iii) **denken** and **bringen** change both the vowel and final consonant of the stem in the imperfect and past participle but have regular weak endings eg:

| infinitive | present | imperfect | past participle |
|---|---|---|---|
| bringen | ich bringe | ich brachte | gebracht |
| denken | ich denke | ich dachte | gedacht *etc* |

The imperfect subjunctive is:

| | | |
|---|---|---|
| ich brächte | ich dächte | *etc* |

iv) **wissen**

wissen forms its main tenses in a similar way to the modal verbs:

| *present* | **ich weiß** |
| | **du weißt** |
| | **er/sie/es weiß** |
| | **wir wissen** |
| | **ihr wisst** |
| | **Sie/sie wissen** |

| *imperfect* | **ich wusste** |
| | **du wusstest** |
| | **er/sie/es wusste** |
| | **wir wussten** |
| | **ihr wusstet** |
| | **Sie/sie wussten** |

| *past participle* | **gewusst** |

| *present subjunctive* | **ich wisse** |
| | **du wissest** |
| | **er/sie/es wisse** |
| | **wir wissen** |
| | **ihr wisset** |
| | **Sie/sie wissen** |

| *imperfect subjunctive* | **ich wüsste** |
| | **du wüsstest** |
| | **er/sie/es wüsste** |
| | **wir wüssten** |
| | **ihr wüsstet** |
| | **Sie/sie wüssten** |

v) A small number of verbs have parallel weak and strong forms, sometimes with a difference in sense between the two forms.

Many are not commonly needed for everyday use but two more common examples are noted here:

| | |
|---|---|
| bewegen (bewegte, bewegt) | = to move |
| bewegen (bewog, bewogen) | = to persuade someone (to do something) |
| schaffen (schaffte, geschafft) | = to do, achieve |
| schaffen (schuf, geschaffen) | = to create |

vi) some verbs have a combination of strong and weak forms:

| mahlen | mahlte | gemahlen |
|---|---|---|
| salzen | salzte | gesalzen |

In some cases a more modern weak form is replacing an older strong one:

backen - backte *(older:* buk) - gebacken

 **B NOTES ON VERB FORMS**

## 1 The formation of compound tenses with haben or sein

a) haben *is used*

i) with all transitive verbs, ie verbs that can take an object:

**er hat die Wurst gegessen**
he ate the sausage

This applies even where the verb is used without an object:

**er hat schon gegessen**
he has already eaten

The few exceptions are transitive verbs formed by adding a prefix to a verb that normally takes sein:

**er ist seinen Husten noch nicht losgeworden**
he hasn't got rid of his cough yet

ii) with intransitive verbs denoting activity:

**du hast aber fleißig gearbeitet**
you have been working hard

iii) with all reflexive verbs:

**hast du dich schon gewaschen?**
have you washed yet?

iv) with modal verbs:

**mein Sohn hat den Film nicht sehen können**
my son couldn't see the film

**das habe ich nicht gewollt**
that wasn't my intention

**solche Musik habe ich immer gemocht**
I've always liked that kind of music

v) with impersonal verbs:

**es hat geregnet**
it rained

except:

| | | | |
|---|---|---|---|
| gelingen | misslingen | glücken | missglücken |
| geschehen | passieren | vorkommen | widerfahren |

**es ist ihm gelungen**          **es ist schon passiert, dass ...**
he succeeded                          it's happened before that ...

except impersonal expressions with verbs that normally take **sein**:

**wie ist es dir ergangen?**
how did you get on?

b) **sein** *is used*

i) with intransitive verbs expressing change of place, state or
situation. The most frequently used verbs of this type are those
expressing motion from one place to another:

**er ist nach Hause gegangen**          **das Geld ist verschwunden**
he has gone home                             the money's disappeared

**das Haus ist abgebrannt**
the house has burnt down

ii) with the verbs listed as exceptions of v above, whether used impersonally or not:

**der Plan ist missglückt**
the plan failed

iii) with **sein** and **werden** used both as auxiliary verbs and as full verbs:

**das wäre besser gewesen**     **die Milch ist sauer geworden**
that would have been better     the milk has gone off

**der Vorschlag ist akzeptiert worden**
the suggestion has been accepted

c) *verbs which may take either* **sein** *or* **haben***:*

i) Note that many verbs of motion can form their perfect tense with **sein** or **haben**, depending on the sense. Motion from one place to another requires **sein**, motion seen as a way of spending time takes **haben**:

**sie sind nach Griechenland gesegelt**
they sailed to Greece

**im Urlaub hat er jeden Tag gesegelt**
on holiday he went sailing every day

There is a modern tendency not to make this distinction:

**wir sind über den See geschwommen**
we swam across the lake

and:

**wir sind den ganzen Tag geschwommen**
we swam all day

instead of:

**wir haben den ganzen Tag geschwommen**
we swam all day

The latter is still perfectly correct, however.

Verbs which still normally keep this distinction in usage between **sein** and **haben** are:

| **paddeln** | **reiten** | **rudern** | **segeln** | **tanzen** |
|---|---|---|---|---|
| to paddle | to ride | to row | to sail | to dance |

ii) Some verbs of motion can be used both transitively and intransitively; in the first case they are conjugated with **haben**, in the second with **sein**:

**gestern hat er den Wagen gefahren**
he drove the car yesterday

**sie ist nach Hause gefahren**
she drove home

**er hat das Rohr gebogen**
he bent the pipe

**sie ist um die Ecke gebogen**
she went round the corner

iii) Note similar distinctions:

**er ist mir gefolgt**
he followed me

**er hat mir gefolgt**
he obeyed me

**der See ist gefroren**
the lake has frozen

**ich habe gefroren**
I was freezing

iv) As a rule, **liegen**, **sitzen** and **stehen** are conjugated with **haben** in north Germany and with **sein** in south Germany and Austria.

## 2 The order of infinitives and past participles

a) In tenses formed with an auxiliary verb – **sein**, **haben**, **werden** and the modals – the auxiliary verb comes in second position in the sentence but the past participle and/or infinitive comes at the end of the clause:

**wir sind gestern gefahren**
we travelled yesterday

**das kann ich nicht sagen**
I can't say

**es wird gerade gebaut**
it's just being built

**b)** If there is both a past participle and an infinitive, the past participle comes first:

**sie werden früher gefahren sein**
they must have gone earlier

**c)** The infinitive of a modal verb used as a past participle and the past participle of **werden** come after the infinitive or past participle of the main verb:

**das hättest du voraussehen können**
you should have foreseen that

**es ist noch nicht gebaut worden**
it hasn't been built yet

**d)** In the future perfect passive the past participle is followed by **worden** and then **sein**:

**es wird sicher bis Montag gefunden worden sein**
I'm sure it will have been found by Monday

**e)** In the future perfect plus a modal verb the past participle is followed by the infinitive of **sein** or **haben** and then the infinitive of the modal:

**er wird es gefunden haben müssen**
he will have had to have found it

Note that these last two forms are often regarded as clumsy (*see* **p 129**).

**f)** Special word order in subordinate clauses

When two infinitive forms occur in a subordinate clause then the finite verb comes before them:

**weißt du, dass ich dich habe kommen sehen?**
do you know I saw you coming?

**er sagte, dass er mich nicht hat verstehen können**
he said he hadn't been able to understand me

## 3 Prefixes

a) *inseparable*

The inseparable prefixes are:

be    emp    ent    er    ge    miss    ver    zer

In pronunciation they are not stressed. They never separate from the verb. A verb with such a prefix has no ge- in the past participle.

b) *separable*

i) All other common prefixes are separable with the exception of the group mentioned in c) below. When they are attached to the verb they are stressed in pronunciation.

In statements, questions and imperatives these prefixes separate from the verb and are placed at the end of the clause. This does not apply in subordinate clauses where the finite verb is also at the end. In these cases the prefix and verb are joined:

**kommst du mit?**               **kommen Sie mit!**
are you coming?             come with me

**sie fangen an**
they're beginning

*but:*  **weißt du, wann sie anfangen?**
      do you know when they begin?

ii) The past participle for verbs with a separable prefix is formed with the ge coming between the prefix and verb stem:

**anfangen – angefangen**        **beibringen – beigebracht**

iii) When a verb with a separable prefix is in the infinitive form and is used with zu, the zu comes between the prefix and the verb stem:

**er versuchte, den Weg abzukürzen**
he tried to take a short cut

**um die Zeit gut auszunutzen**
so as to make good use of the time

c) *separable or inseparable*

durch    hinter    über    um    unter    wider    voll

can be either separable or inseparable prefixes. In most such cases the separable and inseparable verbs have different meanings:

**der Gärtner gräbt den Dung unter**
the gardener digs the dung in

*but:*

**er untergräbt seine Gesundheit**
he is undermining his health

Usually the separable verb has a concrete, physical meaning, the inseparable verb a figurative meaning.

wieder is always separable except in wiederholen in the sense of 'to repeat':

**ich habe sie nie wiedergesehen**    **sie wiederholten die Lektion**
I never saw her again           they repeated the lesson

d) *double prefixes*

i) In verbs which already have an inseparable prefix to which a separable one is added (eg ab-be-rufen) the separable prefix still separates, the zu is inserted between separable and inseparable prefix *but* the past participle has no ge-:

**die Regierung beruft den Botschafter ab**
the government recalls its ambassador

**die Regierung beabsichtigt, den Botschafter abzuberufen**
the government intends to recall its ambassador

**der Botschafter wurde abberufen**
the ambassador was recalled

ii) Verbs formed by the combination of inseparable prefix + separable prefix + verb (eg be-ab-sichtigen) are inseparable:

**er beabsichtigt, morgen zu kommen**
he intends to come tomorrow

## C USE OF TENSES AND MOODS

**1** The present tense

a) The present tense is used

   i) to express present states or actions:

     **ich fühle mich schlecht**      **der Arzt gibt mir eine Spritze**
     I feel ill      the doctor is giving me an injection

   ii) to express general or universal truths:

     **Sabine hört gern Rockmusik**      **Zeit ist Geld**
     Sabine likes listening to rock music      time is money

   iii) for firm intentions, refusals and for orders as an alternative to the imperative:

     **ich mache das**      **das Auto springt nicht an**
     I'll do it      the car won't start
     **du gehst sofort ins Bett!**
     you're to go to bed at once
     **ich bleibe keine Minute länger hier!**
     I won't stay here a minute longer

     This tense is often translated by either the English present or the present continuous:

     **es regnet jeden Tag**      **es regnet**
     it rains every day      it is raining

b) In German the present tense is the most common way of expressing the future:

**ich bin gleich zurück**      **nächste Woche ist alles vorbei**
I'll be right back      it'll all be over by next week
**du bekommst einen Brief**
you'll be getting a letter

c) With the conjunctions **seit** and **seitdem** and adverbial phrases using the preposition **seit** the present tense is used to express actions or states starting in the past and continuing into the present:

**seit(dem) er die Tabletten nimmt, geht es ihm viel besser**
since he has been taking the tablets he has been much better

**er wartet seit zehn Uhr**
he has been waiting since ten o'clock

d) The historic present is more common in German than in English. It is used to enliven a narrative of past events in written or spoken German:

**ich liege auf der Couch - da kommt der Peter und gießt mir Wasser über den Kopf**
there I was lying on the sofa when in came Peter and poured water over my head

It is also used for newspaper headlines and historical notes:

**DIE QUEEN BESUCHT BERLIN**
THE QUEEN VISITS BERLIN

**1814: Napoleon entkommt aus der Haft**
1814: Napoleon escapes

## 2 The imperfect tense

a) The imperfect tense is the standard tense for stories, novels and newspaper reports.

**er ging die Straße entlang**
he went along the road

**der russische Außenminister traf gestern in Berlin ein**
the Russian foreign minister arrived in Berlin yesterday

b) The imperfect tense is the one most commonly used (less so in southern Germany) with **sein**, **haben** and the modal verbs when referring to the past:

**das war klasse!**                    **ich konnte es kaum glauben**
that was great!                        I could hardly believe it

c) Note the following use of the imperfect with **seit(dem)**:

> **seit(dem) er in Hamburg wohnte, hatte er ...**
> since he had been living in Hamburg, he had ...

## 3 The perfect tense

The perfect tense is the standard tense for conversation when talking about the past (except when using **haben**, **sein** and the modals as shown in 2.):

> **hast du ihn gesehen?**          **wann ist sie angekommen?**
> did you see him?                      when did she arrive?

This does not mean to say that the imperfect cannot be used in German conversation. If, for example, you are relating a series of events then it is quite in order to use the imperfect (it's like telling a story). But for single utterances as in the above two examples, the use of the imperfect would sound odd.

## 4 The pluperfect tense

The pluperfect is used for events that happened before a particular time in the past:

> **nachdem wir den Film gesehen hatten, gingen wir ins Café**
> after we had seen the film we went to a café

## 5 The future and future perfect tenses

a) The future is used to express future matters but is less common in German than in English (*see* **1b** *above*). The future as in:

> **ich werde ihn morgen treffen**
> I'm going to meet him tomorrow

is very often expressed by the present:

> **ich treffe ihn morgen**
> I'm meeting him tomorrow

b) It is also used to express suppositions about the present:

**er hört mich nicht, er wird das Radio anhaben**
he can't hear me, he's probably got the radio on

c) The future perfect is used to refer to an event that will be completed at some stage in the future:

**ich werde das Buch bis Montag gelesen haben**
I'll have read the book by Monday

It is also commonly used in German to express a supposition as in b) above:

**er wird es vergessen haben**
he'll have forgotten it

## **6** The passive

In the passive the active form ('he did it') is inverted so that the object becomes subject ('it was done by him').

a) There are two forms of the passive in German: the passive of action and the passive of state. The first (formed with **werden**) emphasises the action that was carried out, the second (formed with **sein**) denotes the result:

| **die Vase wurde zerbrochen** | **die Vase ist zerbrochen** |
|---|---|
| the vase was broken | the vase is broken |

When an agent is mentioned (who it was done by) the passive formed with **werden** must be used:

**diese Wohnungen werden von der Stadt gebaut**
these flats are being built by the council

> *but:* **unser Haus ist schon gebaut**
> our house is already built

b) Verbs that take the dative or that are followed by a preposition cannot form the passive in this way and so a passive construction is usually avoided. For example:

**sie sind ihm gefolgt**
he was followed by them

When a passive is used with such verbs, note the difference from English:

**mir wurde gesagt**
*I* was told

c) Intransitive verbs can be transformed into an impersonal passive in which there is commonly no agent expressed:

**es wurde getanzt**
there was dancing

d) The agent (the subject of the verb in its active form) is usually referred to by the preposition von:

**er wurde von seinem besten Freund betrogen**
he was betrayed by his best friend

durch is most often used when the agent is not a person:

**die Ernte wurde durch Hagel vernichtet**
the harvest was destroyed by hail

**ich wurde durch den Verkehr aufgehalten**
I was held up by traffic

e) Note the use of man to replace a passive construction where a sentence such as 'it had been completely forgotten about' can be expressed either by:

**es war völlig vergessen worden**

or by:

**man hatte es völlig vergessen**

f) The passive can also be expressed by lassen:

| | |
|---|---|
| **das lässt sich machen** | **er ließ sich nicht überreden** |
| that can be done | he couldn't be persuaded |

g) The infinitive with zu can also be used to express the passive:

| | |
|---|---|
| **wie ist das zu erklären?** | **er war nicht zu verstehen** |
| how is that to be explained? | he couldn't be understood |

## 7 The imperative

a) The imperative is used to express requests and can range from a peremptory demand to a polite suggestion:

**bleiben Sie stehen!**
stop!

**komm doch her!**
come here!

**sieh dir den kleinen Bengel an!**
just look at the little rascal!

**hören Sie nicht auf!**
don't stop!

There is normally an exclamation mark, even after polite requests.

b) In the wir form, it is used for suggestions:

**gehen wir!**
let's go!

**machen wir es uns gemütlich!**
let's make ourselves comfortable

c) The infinitive is an alternative imperative, usually for fairly peremptory commands, for example in road signs *etc*:

**links fahren!**
drive on the left

**nicht hinauslehnen!**
do not lean out

## 8 The subjunctive

a) In spite of the fact that certain forms of the subjunctive are felt to be stilted (and are often replaced by the indicative or the würde form), it is still widely used in German:

   i) in conversation for conditional statements and with the modal verbs and:

   ii) in formal German, eg news bulletins, for reported statements.

The subjunctive gives the verb a mood of uncertainty, improbability or unreality. Thus it is mainly used for conditional statements, to express what might have been or what might, but probably will not, be; and for reported speech where it shows that what is reported was said by someone else and the speaker is not guaranteeing it to be a true statement.

**b)** The use of the subjunctive in conditional sentences

i) Conditional sentences contain a main clause and an 'if' (**wenn**) clause. Conditional clauses in the present tense do not require the subjunctive; they state what will happen if some condition is fulfilled:

**wenn es morgen regnet, arbeite ich zu Hause**
if it rains tomorrow, I'll work at home

ii) Conditions with the imperfect subjunctive in the main clause and in the **wenn** clause suggest the condition is unlikely to be fulfilled:

**wenn ich mehr Zeit hätte, ginge ich öfter spazieren**
if I had more time, I would go for more walks

iii) The use of the **würde** forms

The verb in the example above could be replaced by a **würde** form (the conditional):

**wenn ich mehr Zeit hätte, würde ich öfter spazieren gehen**
**wäre** and **hätte** are normally preferred to **sein würde** and **haben würde**.

Note the possibility of omitting the **wenn** when there is inversion of subject and verb:

**hätte ich mehr Zeit, ginge ich öfter spazieren**

iv) Conditions with the pluperfect subjunctive in both clauses indicate what might have happened but did not:

**wenn er mich gefragt hätte, hätte ich ihm das Geld geliehen**
if he had asked me, I would have lent him the money

The substitution of **würde** forms is also possible here, though less common.

v) A **wenn** clause with the subjunctive can be used by itself in the sense of 'if only':

**wenn es nur schon Weihnachten wäre**
if only it were Christmas

c) **The subjunctive with als ob and als wenn**

The als ob or als wenn ('as if') construction expresses something which is regarded as uncertain or misleading and normally uses the subjunctive, although in spoken German the indicative can be used:

**er tut, als ob er uns nicht gesehen hätte**
he behaves as if he hadn't seen us

d) The subjunctive can be used in a main clause alone for instructions in mathematics and cookery:

**man nehme fünf Eier**
take five eggs

and with leben meaning 'long live' or 'three cheers for'

| **es lebe die Revolution!** | **er lebe hoch!** |
| long live the revolution! | three cheers for him! |

e) The subjunctive can also be used for questions and requests to make them less blunt and therefore more polite:

| **ich hätte eine Frage** | **hätten Sie fünf Minuten für mich?** |
| might I ask a question? | could you spare me five minutes? |

f) The subjunctive can be used for suggestions in the phrase wie wäre es mit ... ('how about ...?'):

**wie wär's mit einem Glas Wein?**
how about a glass of wine?

g) For the idiomatic uses of the subjunctive of modal verbs, see the section on modal verbs below.

h) **The subjunctive in indirect speech**

i) Indirect speech is the name given to statements or questions spoken by one person and reported by someone else:
he said, 'I will go there' → he said he would go there

The indirect speech is usually contained in a clause following a verb of speaking or asking. In German, such clauses are the only ones where the introductory dass may be omitted; if there is no dass normal word order is maintained:

**er sagte, dass er kommen würde**   **er sagte, er würde kommen**
he said he would come                he said he would come

ii) Indirect speech without the subjunctive
In German, direct speech is usually put into indirect speech by using the subjunctive, but if the verb of saying or asking is in the present tense, then the indicative is more common:

**er sagt, dass er kommt**
he says he's coming

In colloquial German the subjunctive is often avoided and the indicative retained in the tense used in direct speech:

**er hat gesagt, dass er kommt**
he said he would come

iii) Indirect speech with the subjunctive
The choice of tense for the indirect statement depends on the tense of the original direct speech as shown in the following table:

| indicative tense of direct speech | subjunctive tense of indirect speech |
| --- | --- |
| present | present, imperfect |
| imperfect, perfect or pluperfect | perfect, pluperfect |
| future | future, würde + infinitive |

*Examples*

| | |
| --- | --- |
| **ich finde es schwierig**<br>I find it difficult | **er hat gesagt, er finde/fände es schwierig**<br>he said he found it difficult |
| **ich fand es schwierig**<br>**ich habe es schwierig gefunden**<br>**ich hatte es schwierig gefunden** | **er hat gesagt, er habe/hätte es schwierig gefunden** |

ich werde es schwierig finden  er hat gesagt, er werde/würde es
schwierig finden

iv) The choice of subjunctive tense in indirect speech

Written German

The preferred tenses in formal written German are the
present subjunctive, the imperfect subjunctive and the future
subjunctive (the first ones given in each of the examples above).

The main exceptions occur when the form of the subjunctive
is identical to the indicative form it is replacing. In such
cases the alternative form given above is used:

sie sagten, sie fänden (*not* finden) es schwierig
sie sagten, sie hätten (*not* haben) es schwierig gefunden
sie sagten, sie würden (*not* werden) es schwierig finden

If the present and imperfect subjunctives are both the same
as the indicatives, the imperfect subjunctive is preferred:

sie sagten, sie arbeiteten (*not* arbeiten) fleißig

Spoken German

The preferred tenses in spoken German are the imperfect
subjunctive, pluperfect subjunctive and würde + infinitive
forms (the second choices given in the examples above).

The würde + infinitive form is very commonly used instead of
the imperfect subjunctive for verbs other than sein and haben:

sie sagte: "Ich wohne hier"  sie sagte, sie würde hier wohnen

she said, "I live here"  she said she lived here

# 9 The uses of the infinitive

The infinitive can be used together with certain verbs without any
connecting link; in all other cases it is connected to the verb, noun
or adjective phrase with zu.

a) *the infinitive without* zu

The infinitive is used without zu with modal verbs, and with certain verbs of perception, causation and instruction:

| | |
|---|---|
| dürfen | to be allowed to |
| können | to be able to |
| mögen | to like to |
| müssen | to have to |
| sollen | to be supposed to |
| wollen | to want to |
| fühlen | to feel |
| hören | to hear |
| sehen | to see |
| spüren | to feel |
| heißen | to order to |
| lassen | to make, cause to; to allow to |
| machen | to make |
| helfen | to help to |
| lehren | to teach to |
| lernen | to learn to |

i) modals

**ich darf das nicht tun**
I'm not allowed to do that

**er will es gesehen haben**
he claims to have seen it

**das muss heute getan werden**
it has to be done today

ii) The verbs of perception, causation and instruction normally have an object (in the dative with helfen) as well as the infinitive:

**er fühlte sein Herz schlagen**
he felt his heart beating

**hörst du ihn kommen?**
can you hear him coming?

**ich sah ihn fallen**
I saw him fall

**er machte die Leute aufhorchen**
he made the people sit up and listen

**er spürte eine Wut in sich aufsteigen**
he felt his anger rising

**er hieß die Soldaten warten** (*literary German*)
he told the soldiers to wait
**sie ließ die Schüler früh nach Hause gehen**
she allowed the children to go home early
**Montag lasse ich den Wagen waschen**
on Monday I'll get the car washed
**sie haben mir aufräumen geholfen**     **wer hat dich schwimmen gelehrt?**
they helped me tidy up     who taught you to swim?
**er lernt gerade Auto fahren**
he's just learning to drive

---

## Note

When helfen, lehren and lernen are followed by an infinitive which
has its own object or an adverb with it, the tendency is to use zu.

*Compare:*

**der Blindenhund hilft ihm gehen**
the guide dog helps him to walk

*and:*

**der Blindenhund hilft ihm, die Straße zu überqueren**
the guide dog helps him to cross the road

---

iii) The infinitive after lassen (and less commonly after sehen,
hören and heißen) often has a passive sense:

   **er ließ das Zimmer streichen**
   he had the room painted

   Compare this with the following use of lassen:

   **er ließ mich das Zimmer streichen**
   he got me to paint the room

   lassen is used in this way as a reflexive (*see* **p 167**):

   **das lässt sich machen**
   that can be done

iv) After bleiben, verbs of sitting, standing, lying *etc* are in the infinitive without zu:

**bleib sitzen!**          **er blieb auf dem Boden liegen**
stay seated          he remained lying on the ground

v) brauchen is normally used with zu + infinitive in standard German but is also sometimes used without zu, especially in spoken German:

**das brauchst du nicht an(zu)nehmen**
you don't have to accept that

vi) kommen, gehen and schicken are used without zu with verbs denoting activities:

**kommst du morgen schwimmen?**
are you coming swimming tomorrow?

**er hat die Kinder einkaufen geschickt**
he sent the children out shopping

## Note

- Past participle: when heißen, lassen, sehen and hören are used together with another infinitive, then it is normal to use the infinitive forms (heißen, lassen, sehen, hören) rather than the past participle forms (geheißen, gelassen, gesehen, gehört):

**er hat mich kommen sehen**
he saw me coming
**er hat das Feuer ausgehen lassen**
he let the fire go out

- Special word order: in subordinate clauses the finite verb precedes two infinitives at the end of a sentence:

**weil er dich hat kommen lassen**
because he got you to come

b) *the infinitive with* zu

  i) After nouns:

   **hast du Lust mitzuspielen?**
   would you like to join in the game?

  ii) After adjectives:

   **ich war froh, ihn gesehen zu haben**
   I was glad to have seen him

  iii) After past participles:

   **er war erstaunt, mich zu sehen**
   he was astonished to see me

  iv) After the prepositions um, (an)statt, and ohne:

   um ... zu is used to express purpose:

   **er zahlte mehr, um einen besseren Platz zu bekommen**
   he paid more to get a better seat

   um ... zu is also used after genug ('enough') and zu ('too') +
   adjective:

   **du bist alt genug, um das zu wissen**
   you're old enough to know that

   **er ist zu schwach, um Nein zu sagen**
   he's too weak to say no

   (an)statt zu ('instead of'):

   **(an)statt zu feuern, ließ er die Waffe fallen**
   he dropped his gun instead of shooting

   ohne zu ('without')

   **er ging vorbei, ohne zu grüßen**
   he went past without saying hello

   Note that after nouns, adjectives, past participles and
   prepositions the subject of the main verb must also be the
   subject of the infinitive.

v) After verbs:

**es begann sofort zu regnen**     **wir versuchten ihn aufzuhalten**
it immediately started to rain     we tried to stop him

Verbs which are followed by a preposition often, but not always, have **da(r)** + preposition before the **zu** + infinitive phrase:

**ich freue mich darauf, euch zu sehen**
I'm looking forward to seeing you

**er ärgerte sich (darüber), den Zug verpasst zu haben**
he was annoyed at missing the train

After **sein** the infinitive with **zu** has a passive meaning:

**er ist nicht zu ersetzen**     **der Schmerz war nicht zu ertragen**
he is irreplaceable     the pain was unbearable

vi) *For the punctuation of the infinitival clause see* **pp 250-251**

c) *For the use of the infinitive as imperative see* **section 7c** *above.*

d) The infinitive can also be used as a noun. Such nouns begin with a capital letter and are always neuter; they generally denote the action of the verb:

**das Schwimmen**
swimming

They can be compounded with a noun object:

**das Autofahren**
car driving

They are often used with **bei**:

**er wurde beim Mogeln ertappt**
he was caught cheating

## 10   The uses of the participles

a) *present participle*

i) The present participle is used mainly as an adjective either before the noun or after **sein**:

**eine ansteckende Krankheit**     **diese Krankheit ist ansteckend**
an infectious disease     this disease is infectious

ii) It can occasionally be used as an adverb after other verbs:

**sie redete überzeugend**
she talked convincingly

iii) The present participle preceded by zu – which can have further words or phrases before it – can be used as an extended adjective before the noun:

**kein einfach zu lösendes Problem**
a problem that is/was not easy to solve

**eine schwer zu begreifende Entscheidung**
a decision that is/was difficult to comprehend

iv) Phrases using present participles in the following way mainly occur in literary usage:

**die Zeitung zerknüllend, stand er auf**
crumpling the paper, he stood up

b) *past participle*

i) Apart from its use to form tenses, the past participle is also used as an adjective:

**der verdammte Bengel**
that damned rascal

ii) Its use to form extended adjective phrases before the noun is widespread in formal written German:

**der erst neulich gestürzte Präsident**
the recently deposed president

iii) Phrases using past participles in the following way mainly occur in literary usage:

**vom Einbruch der Nacht überrascht, musste er im Freien schlafen**
being suddenly overtaken by nightfall, he had to sleep out of doors

*but:*

a small number of verbs are in common use in such participial constructions, for example: **vorausgesetzt, gesagt, ausgenommen**:

**genau gesagt**
to be precise

**dein Bruder ausgenommen, fahren alle mit dem Zug**
except for your brother everyone is going by train

iv) The past participle is used idiomatically with kommen:

**er kam gelaufen**
he came running

## 11 The usages of modal verbs (*conjugation see* pp 127-31)

a) dürfen

i) dürfen expresses permission ('to be allowed to'):

**niemand darf das Haus verlassen**
no-one may leave the house

**darf ich Sie stören?**　　　　　　**das darfst du nicht sagen**
may I interrupt?　　　　　　　　　you shouldn't/mustn't say that

ii) dürfen in the imperfect subjunctive expresses a probable supposition:

**er dürfte gestern krank gewesen sein**
he was probably ill yesterday

**das dürfte wohl stimmen**
that might well be true

iii) dürfen in the negative translates English 'must not':

**du darfst nicht bei Rot über die Straße gehen**
you must not cross the road when the lights are red

iv) Idiomatic uses:

**was darf es sein?**
*(in shop)* what can I do for you?
*(getting a drink)* what can I get you?

b) können

i) können expresses ability:

**er kann gut schwimmen**　　　　　**kannst du Spanisch?**
he can swim well　　　　　　　　　can you speak Spanish?

**kannst du Gitarre spielen?**
do you know how to play the guitar?

**leider können wir nicht kommen**
I'm afraid we can't come

ii) **können** expresses possibility:

**er kann den Einbrecher gesehen haben**
he might have seen the burglar

**du kannst recht haben**
you might be right

iii) **können** is often used in place of **dürfen** to express permission, especially in spoken German:

**du kannst machen, was du willst**
you can do as you like

iv) **können** is used in the idiom **etwas/jemand (gut) leiden können**:

**ich kann diese Musik gut leiden**
I like this music

c) **mögen**

Note that **mögen** is also used with an object, meaning 'to like':

**ich mag keine Rockmusik**
I don't like rock music

i) The commonest use of **mögen** is to express wish or desire. In this usage it is most often seen in the imperfect subjunctive:

**ich möchte ihn kennenlernen**    **ich möchte ein Eis**
I'd like to get to know him    I'd like an ice cream

but it is also used in the present:

**ich mag nicht länger bleiben**
I don't want to stay any longer

ii) **mögen** is used to express supposition or possibility:

**du magst recht haben**    **wer mag das sein?**
you may well be right    who can/might that be?

**er mochte etwa zwanzig sein**
he was probably about twenty

iii) **mögen** expresses concession:

**das mag sein, aber es gefällt mir nicht**
that may be so, but I don't like it

iv) The imperfect subjunctive of **mögen** is also used as a polite alternative to the imperative:

**Besucher möchten das Schloss bitte vor sechs Uhr verlassen**
visitors are asked to leave the castle before six o'clock

v) It is used in the idiom **jemand (gut) leiden mögen**:

**ich mag ihn gut leiden**
I like him

d) **müssen**

i) **müssen** is used to express necessity:

**ich muss schon sagen ...**    **ich musste mich beeilen**
I really must say ...    I had to hurry

ii) It can also express supposition:

**jemand muss es versteckt haben**
someone must have hidden it

iii) In the imperfect subjunctive it expresses a wish or hope:

**das müsste eigentlich passen**    **Geld müsste man haben!**
that ought to fit    it would be nice to have money

iv) The negative of **müssen** is not the same as 'must not' in English:

**du musst nicht kommen**
you don't have to come

In order to say 'you must not come', German uses **dürfen**:

**du darfst nicht kommen**
you must not come

e) **sollen**

i) **sollen** expresses duty or obligation:

**du sollst nicht töten**    **er sollte seinem Vater helfen**
thou shalt not kill    he ought to help his father
**ich hätte es früher tun sollen**
I ought to have done it earlier

> ## Note
>
> There is sometimes a distinction in this sense between the present
> and the imperfect subjunctive. The present tense implies that
> the obligation is imposed from the outside while the imperfect
> subjunctive implies that it comes from within the speaker:
>
> **ich soll nicht rauchen**  **ich sollte nicht rauchen**
> I shouldn't smoke          I shouldn't smoke
> *(= my doctor's told me)*  *(= I know it's bad for me)*

ii) sollen is used to express a rumour or generally held opinion:

**dieser soll der beste sein**
this one is supposed to be the best

**es sollte heute regnen, hat aber nicht**
it was supposed to rain today but didn't

iii) The imperfect tense of sollen can be used to express a future in
the past:

**das sollte ihn teuer zu stehen kommen**
he was to pay dearly for it

**das sollten wir später erfahren**
we were to find that out later

f) wollen

i) wollen expresses intention or desire:

**er will nur dein Bestes**       **ich will sie heiraten**
he only wants the best for you    I'm determined to marry her

Note the use of wollen with non-personal subjects in the sense
of 'to refuse to':

**der Regen wollte nicht enden**   **der Motor wollte nicht anspringen**
the rain just wouldn't stop        the engine refused to start

Note the construction with dass:

**alle wollen, dass du kommst**    **er will, dass ich ihm helfe**
everyone wants you to come         he wants me to help him

ii) **wollen** is used to express a claim made by someone and reported by the speaker:

**er will das Geld gar nicht gesehen haben**
he claims he never saw the money

**er will alles besser wissen**
he always thinks he knows best

iii) In the imperfect tense and followed by **gerade** it is the equivalent of 'to be about to':

**er wollte gerade verschwinden**
he was about to disappear

iv) **wollen** is used with the passive infinitive in the sense of 'must':

**der Fall will vorsichtig behandelt werden**
the case must be handled carefully

g) *The omission of the infinitive with the modal verb*

Infinitives expressing movement may be omitted when it is clear what is intended; this is usually when there is an adverb or adverbial phrase expressing direction:

**du sollst sofort in die Schule**
you are to go to school at once

**ich muss heute nach Dortmund**
I have to go to Dortmund today

**ich darf nicht nach draußen**
I'm not allowed out

h) *The alternative perfect and pluperfect forms of the modal verbs often have different meanings.*

**er hat es tun sollen**
he was supposed to do it

**er soll es getan haben**
he is supposed to have done it

**er hat es tun müssen**
he had to do it

**er muss es getan haben**
he must have done it

With **können** the distinction is less obvious from the English:

**er hat es tun können**
he could have done it
*(= had the opportunity)*

**er kann es getan haben**
he may have done it
*(= is a possible culprit)*

> **er hätte es tun können**
> he could have done it
> *(= if he had been willing)*

> **er könnte es getan haben**
> he might have done it
> *(= is a possible culprit)*

## 12 Impersonal verbs

a) Impersonal verbs are verbs which have **es** as the subject when **es** does not refer to any specific person, thing or action.

*Compare*:

**es ist besser zu gehen**
it's better to go (impersonal)

*and*:

**dieses Buch? –es ist mein Lieblingsbuch**
this book? –it's my favourite ('personal', **es** refers to the book)

Impersonal verbs can be divided into two groups, depending on whether the **es** is kept when the subject and verb are inverted:

> **es gibt kein Essen heute**
> **heute gibt's kein Essen**
> there's no food today

> **es ist mir schlecht**
> **mir ist schlecht**
> I feel ill

b) Apart from those listed under c) below, impersonal verbs and expressions retain the **es** in inversion. In some cases the **es** in inversion is optional. Below are some of the main types of impersonal verbs that keep the **es**:

Verbs of weather and similar phenomena:

| | | |
|---|---|---|
| **es regnet**<br>it's raining | **es schneit**<br>it's snowing | **es hagelt**<br>it's hailing |
| **es donnert**<br>it's thundering | **es blitzt**<br>there is lightning | **es friert**<br>it's freezing |
| **es dunkelt**<br>it's getting dark | **es tagt**<br>it's getting light | **es dämmert**<br>dawn/twilight is coming |
| **es wird Sommer**<br>summer is coming | **es spukt**<br>there are ghosts about | |
| **es brennt**<br>there's a fire | **es zieht**<br>there's a draught | |

Note that some of these may be used to refer to persons:

| | |
|---|---|
| **es friert mich** | **es ist mir kalt** |
| I'm freezing | I'm cold |

This form is felt to be slightly stilted and inversion is common:

| | |
|---|---|
| **mich friert (es)** | **mir ist (es) kalt** |

The **es** may be kept but is usually omitted.

Verbs of noise:

| | |
|---|---|
| **es klingelt** | there's a ring |
| **es läutet** | there's a ring |
| **es klopft** | there's a knock |
| **es raschelt** | there's a rustling |

Other impersonal verbs:

| | |
|---|---|
| **es gefällt mir** | I like it |
| **es geht** | it's all right |
| **es gibt** | there is/are |
| **es handelt sich um** | it is a matter of |
| **es kommt darauf an** | it depends |

Note that **es war einmal** ('once upon a time') is never inverted.

c) Impersonal verbs where **es** is omitted in inversion

In expressions formed with **es ist** + adjectives expressing a state of mind, body or health the **es** is normally omitted in inversion:

| | |
|---|---|
| **ihm war traurig zumute** | he felt sad |
| **mir ist warm** | I feel warm |
| **mir wird besser** | I'm getting better |
| **ihr ist schlecht** | she feels sick |

In the impersonal passive the **es** is always omitted in inversion:

**die ganze Nacht hindurch wurde getanzt**
the dancing went on all night

Verbs indicating position omit the **es** in inversion; the most common are **liegen, sein** and **stehen**:

**es steht in der Zeitung, dass ...**
**in der Zeitung steht, dass ...**
it says in the paper that ...

d) es gibt *or* es ist?

es gibt is the usual German translation for 'there is/are'; the verb is always in the singular:

**gibt es einen Aufzug?**
is there a lift?

**zum Abendessen gibt es Forellen**
there is trout for dinner

**es gibt nie Ruhe hier**
there's never any peace and quiet here

es ist/sind is only used when there is an indication of place or position.
*Compare*:

**es ist Post da**
the post has arrived

*and*:

**heute gibt es keine Post**
there's no post today

es ist/sind is particularly common when the presence is only temporary:

**es sind zwei Mädchen an der Tür**
there are two girls at the door

Note that es ist/sind loses the es in inversion:

**in München war eine Demonstration**
there was a demonstration in Munich

es ist/sind can be used for weather, but es gibt is also possible:

**es war diesen Sommer wenig Sonne**
**es hat diesen Sommer wenig Sonne gegeben**
there wasn't much sun this summer

## 13 Reflexive verbs

a) Reflexive verbs are verbs used with a reflexive pronoun which relates the action back to the subject:

I washed myself: 'myself' is the reflexive pronoun.

b) German has both accusative and dative reflexive pronouns:

| PERSON | ACCUSATIVE | DATIVE |
|--------|-----------|--------|
| ich | mich | mir |
| du | dich | dir |
| er/sie/es | sich | sich |
| wir | uns | uns |
| ihr | euch | euch |
| Sie/sie | sich | sich |

There are some German verbs which only occur as reflexives but for which the English equivalent contains no reflexive pronoun:

**beeil dich!**
hurry up!

**ich habe mich dazu entschlossen**
I have decided to do it

c) The position of the reflexive pronoun

The reflexive pronoun usually comes immediately after the verb:

**mein Vater erinnert sich daran**
my father remembers it

With inversion or when the finite verb is at the end it usually follows a pronoun subject but comes before a noun subject or other pronouns:

**erinnert sich dein Vater daran?**
does your father remember it?

**erinnert er sich daran?**
does he remember it?

**erinnert sich einer daran?**
does anyone remember it?

In an infinitive phrase the reflexive pronoun comes first:

**ich muss nicht vergessen, mir ein neues Hemd zu kaufen**
I mustn't forget to buy a new shirt

The reflexive cannot precede the finite verb in normal word order.

Note that all reflexive verbs form their perfect tense with **haben**. The conjugation is as for other verbs.

d) Usage

Reflexive pronouns are basically used to relate the action of the verb back to the subject:

**ich wasche mich**                    **du schadest dir dabei bloß selbst**
I wash myself                          you'll only harm yourself

In the plural the reflexive pronoun can be reciprocal and is often translated into English by 'each other':

**wir sehen uns morgen**
we'll see each other tomorrow

This can also be expressed by **einander**:

**sie sehen einander jeden Tag**
they see each other every day

The accusative reflexive pronoun is used with many verbs with the prefix **ver-** to express that the action of the verb has been done wrongly:

**ich habe mich versprochen**          **er hat sich verzählt**
I made a slip of the tongue            he miscounted

e) There is an impersonal reflexive construction which expresses in general whether an activity is pleasant or easy or not:

**in Turnschuhen läuft es sich bequem**
trainers are comfortable to run in

**in einem weichen Bett schläft es sich schlecht**
soft beds are bad for sleeping in

With the reflexive form of lassen the verb following has a passive sense:

**das lässt sich leicht machen**
that's easily done

The dative reflexive can be used to indicate that the object belongs to the subject of the verb:

**ich wasche mir die Hände**          **sie zog sich die Schuhe an**
I wash my hands                      she put her shoes on

The dative reflexive is also used with many verbs to emphasise the subject's interest or involvement in the activity of the verb. In these cases the dative reflexive is usual but not obligatory:

**den Film sehe ich mir bestimmt an**
I'm certainly going to see that film

**du solltest dir einen neuen Wagen kaufen**
you should buy a new car

When a pronoun used with a preposition refers back to the subject the reflexive pronoun must be used. (It is only in the er/sie/es and Sie/sie forms that it is actually different from the regular pronoun):

**vor sich sah er jemand laufen**
he saw someone running in front of him(self)

**er sah jemand hinter ihm**
he saw someone behind him *(- 'him' not the same person as 'he')*

## 14 Verbs taking the dative

a) The dative is used for the indirect object and comes after many verbs of giving, sending, telling. Often the fact that the object is in the dative will be clear from the English equivalent:

**bring mir die Teller!**
bring the plates to me

*But:*

English often omits the 'to' as in: 'bring me the plates'.
German usage is sometimes different from English:

**sagen Sie es mir!**                    **Sie wollten mich sprechen?**
tell me                                  you wanted to speak to me?

b) Many verbs take both a dative and an accusative object:

**er hat mir alles erzählt**
he told me everything

c) Verbs formed with the prefixes bei- and nach- and inseparable
verbs with the prefix ent- with the basic meaning of 'to escape
from' take the dative:

| | |
|---|---|
| **beistehen** | to support |
| **nachgeben** | to give in to |
| **entkommen** | to escape from |

d) Here is a list of many of the more common verbs that take
a dative object. Verbs that fit into the categories above have
largely been omitted:

| | |
|---|---|
| auffallen | to strike, be noticed |
| ausweichen | to get out of the way of |
| befehlen | to order |
| begegnen | to meet |
| danken | to thank |
| dienen | to serve |
| drohen | to threaten |
| empfehlen | to recommend |
| erlauben | to allow |
| fehlen | to be lacking |
| folgen | to follow |
| gefallen | to please |
| gehorchen | to obey |
| gehören | to belong to |

| | |
|---|---|
| gelingen | to succeed |
| genügen | to be enough for |
| glauben | to believe |
| gratulieren | to congratulate |
| helfen | to help |
| misstrauen | to distrust |
| passen | to suit |
| raten | to advise |
| reichen | to be enough for |
| schaden | to harm |
| schmeicheln | to flatter |
| trauen | to trust |
| verbieten | to forbid |
| versichern | to assure |
| vertrauen | to trust |
| verzeihen | to forgive |
| vorstehen | to preside over |
| wehtun | to hurt |
| widersprechen | to contradict |
| widerstehen | to resist |
| zusehen | to watch |
| zustimmen | to agree to |

## 15 Verbs with two accusative objects

A few verbs can be followed by two objects in the accusative. This is almost entirely restricted to kosten ('to cost'), lehren ('to teach'), nennen ('to call') and fragen ('to ask'):

**das kann ihn den Kragen kosten**
that might be his downfall

**er nannte mich einen Dummkopf**
he called me a fool

**sie haben mich Schwieriges gefragt**
they asked me difficult things

## **16** Verbs followed by prepositions

a) Many German verbs are followed by prepositions. Very often these are not the obvious ones from the English equivalent and should be learnt – along with the case if necessary – with the verb:

**ich fürchte mich vor ihm**
I'm afraid of him

Some verbs can be followed by different prepositions, usually with a change of meaning:

**ich freue mich auf die Ferien**
I'm looking forward to the holidays

**sie hat sich über das Geschenk gefreut**
she was pleased with the present

Such verbs often have a noun following the preposition. However, they can also be followed by an infinitive phrase or a subordinate clause – usually a **dass** clause. When they are followed by such an infinitive or clause it is very common to insert the preposition in the main clause with the prefix **da(r)-** before it:

**ich erinnere mich an ihn**
I remember him

**ich erinnere mich daran, ihn gesehen zu haben**
I remember seeing him

b) Here is a list of some of the more common verbs with prepositions:

   i) an + *acc*

   | | |
   |---|---|
   | **denken an** | to think of *(have in one's mind)* |
   | **sich erinnern an** | to remember |
   | **erinnern an** | to remind |
   | **sich gewöhnen an** | to become accustomed to |

ii) an + *dat*

| | |
|---|---|
| es fehlt an | there is a lack of |
| leiden an | to suffer from *(disease)* |

iii) auf + *acc*

| | |
|---|---|
| achtgeben auf | to pay attention to |
| aufpassen auf | to keep an eye on |
| sich beschränken auf | to restrict oneself to |
| sich freuen auf | to look forward to |
| hoffen auf | to hope for |
| reagieren auf | to react to |
| rechnen auf | to count on |
| sich verlassen auf | to rely upon |
| verzichten auf | to renounce |
| warten auf | to wait for |

iv) auf + *dat*

| | |
|---|---|
| bestehen auf | to insist upon |

v) aus + *dat*

| | |
|---|---|
| bestehen aus | to consist of |

vi) für + *acc*

| | |
|---|---|
| sich bedanken für | to say thank you for |
| sich einsetzen für | to do a lot for |
| sich entscheiden für | to decide in favour of |
| halten für | to consider |
| sich interessieren für | to be interested in |
| sorgen für | to look after |

vii) mit + *dat*

| | |
|---|---|
| aufhören mit | to stop doing |
| einverstanden sein mit | to be in agreement with |
| rechnen mit | to count on |

viii) nach + *dat*

| | |
|---|---|
| fragen nach | to ask for |
| schmecken nach | to taste of |
| suchen nach | to look for |

ix) über + *acc*

| | |
|---|---|
| **sich freuen über** | to be pleased at |
| **lachen über** | to laugh at |
| **nachdenken über** | to reflect upon |

x) um + *acc*

| | |
|---|---|
| **sich kümmern um** | to care for |
| **sich sorgen um** | to be worried about |
| **es geht um** | it is a matter of |
| **es handelt sich um** | it is a matter of |

xi) unter + *dat*

| | |
|---|---|
| **leiden unter** | to suffer from *(noise etc)* |
| **verstehen unter** | to understand by |

xii) von + *dat*

| | |
|---|---|
| **abhängen von** | to be dependent on |
| **sich erholen von** | to recuperate from |
| **handeln von** | to be about |

xiii) vor + *dat*

| | |
|---|---|
| **sich fürchten vor** | to be afraid of |

xiv) zu + *dat*

| | |
|---|---|
| **beitragen zu** | to contribute to |
| **sich entschließen zu** | to decide upon |

## **17** List of strong verbs

Verbs with an asterisk (*) are conjugated with sein.

Verbs with a prefix take the same forms as the simple verbs (without the prefix), eg versprechen and aussprechen take the same forms as sprechen.

Past participles used after infinitives: er hätte nicht bleiben wollen (he wouldn't have wanted to stay). Compare this with: er hat nicht gewollt (he didn't want to).

| Infinitive | English | Present Indicative *3rd pers sing* | Imperfect Indicative | Past Participle |
|------------|---------|------------------|----------|----------------|
| backen | to bake | bäckt, backt | backte | gebacken |
| befehlen | to order | befiehlt | befahl | befohlen |
| beginnen | to begin | beginnt | begann | begonnen |
| beißen | to bite | beißt | biss | gebissen |
| bergen | to salvage, rescue | birgt | barg | geborgen |
| bersten | to burst | birst | barst | geborsten* |
| bewegen | to persuade | bewegt | bewog | bewogen |
| biegen | to bend, turn | biegt | bog | gebogen |
| bieten | to offer | bietet | bot | geboten |
| binden | to tie | bindet | band | gebunden |
| bitten | to ask | bittet | bat | gebeten |
| blasen | to blow | bläst | blies | geblasen |
| bleiben | to stay | bleibt | blieb | geblieben* |
| braten | to fry | brät | briet | gebraten |
| brechen | to break | bricht | brach | gebrochen |
| brennen | to burn | brennt | brannte | gebrannt |
| bringen | to bring | bringt | brachte | gebracht |
| denken | to think | denkt | dachte | gedacht |
| dreschen | to thresh | drischt | drosch | gedroschen |
| dringen | to penetrate, urge | dringt | drang | gedrungen* |
| dürfen | to be allowed to | darf | durfte | gedurft; *(after infinitive)* dürfen |
| empfangen | to receive | empfängt | empfing | empfangen |
| empfehlen | to recommend | empfiehlt | empfahl | empfohlen |
| empfinden | to feel | empfindet | empfand | empfunden |
| erschrecken | to be startled | erschreckt | erschrak | erschrocken* |
| essen | to eat | isst | aß | gegessen |
| fahren | to drive | fährt | fuhr | gefahren* |

173

| fallen | to fall | fällt | fiel | gefallen* |
|--------|---------|-------|------|-----------|
| fangen | to catch | fängt | fing | gefangen |
| fechten | to fence | ficht | focht | gefochten |
| finden | to find | findet | fand | gefunden |
| flechten | to weave, twine | flicht | flocht | geflochten |
| fliegen | to fly | fliegt | flog | geflogen* |
| fliehen | to flee | flieht | floh | geflohen* |
| fließen | to flow | fließt | floss | geflossen* |
| fressen | to eat | frisst | fraß | gefressen |
| frieren | to freeze | friert | fror | gefroren |
| gebären | to give birth (to) | gebiert | gebar | geboren |
| geben | to give | gibt | gab | gegeben |
| gedeihen | to thrive | gedeiht | gedieh | gediehen* |
| gehen | to go | geht | ging | gegangen* |
| gelingen | to succeed | gelingt | gelang | gelungen* |
| gelten | to be valid | gilt | galt | gegolten |
| genesen | to recover, convalesce | genest | genas | genesen* |
| genießen | to enjoy | genießt | genoss | genossen |
| geschehen | to happen | geschieht | geschah | geschehen* |
| gewinnen | to win | gewinnt | gewann | gewonnen |
| gießen | to pour | gießt | goss | gegossen |
| gleichen | to resemble, be like | gleicht | glich | geglichen |
| gleiten | to glide | gleitet | glitt | geglitten* |
| glimmen | to glow | glimmt | glomm | geglommen |
| graben | to dig | gräbt | grub | gegraben |
| greifen | to grasp | greift | griff | gegriffen |
| haben | to have | hat | hatte | gehabt |
| halten | to hold | hält | hielt | gehalten |
| hängen | to hang | hängt | hing | gehangen |
| hauen | to hit, hew | haut | haute | gehauen |
| heben | to lift | hebt | hob | gehoben |
| heißen | to be called | heißt | hieß | geheißen |
| helfen | to help | hilft | half | geholfen |

| kennen | to know | kennt | kannte | gekannt |
|---|---|---|---|---|
| klingen | to sound | klingt | klang | geklungen |
| kneifen | to pinch | kneift | kniff | gekniffen |
| kommen | to come | kommt | kam | gekommen* |
| können | to be able to | kann | konnte | gekonnt; *(after infinitive)* können |
| kriechen | to crawl | kriecht | kroch | gekrochen* |
| laden | to load | lädt | lud | geladen |
| lassen | to leave, let | lässt | ließ | gelassen; *(after infinitive)* lassen |
| laufen | to run | läuft | lief | gelaufen* |
| leiden | to suffer | leidet | litt | gelitten |
| leihen | to lend, borrow | leiht | lieh | geliehen |
| lesen | to read | liest | las | gelesen |
| liegen | to lie | liegt | lag | gelegen |
| lügen | to tell lies | lügt | log | gelogen |
| mahlen | to grind | mahlt | mahlte | gemahlen |
| meiden | to avoid | meidet | mied | gemieden |
| melken | to milk | melkt | melkte | gemolken |
| messen | to measure | misst | maß | gemessen |
| misslingen | to fail | misslingt | misslang | misslungen* |
| mögen | to like | mag | mochte | gemocht; *(after infinitive)* mögen |
| müssen | to have to | muss | musste | gemusst; *(after infinitive)* müssen |
| nehmen | to take | nimmt | nahm | genommen |
| nennen | to call, name | nennt | nannte | genannt |
| pfeifen | to whistle | pfeift | pfiff | gepfiffen |
| preisen | to praise | preist | pries | gepriesen |
| quellen | to pour | quillt | quoll | gequollen* |
| raten | to guess, advise | rät | riet | geraten |
| reiben | to rub | reibt | rieb | gerieben |

| reißen | to rip | reißt | riss | gerissen |
|--------|--------|-------|------|----------|
| reiten | to ride | reitet | ritt | geritten |
| rennen | to run | rennt | rannte | gerannt* |
| riechen | to smell | riecht | roch | gerochen |
| ringen | to wrestle, struggle | ringt | rang | gerungen |
| rinnen | to run *(liquid)* | rinnt | rann | geronnen* |
| rufen | to call | ruft | rief | gerufen |
| salzen | to salt | salzt | salzte | gesalzen |
| saufen | to drink | säuft | soff | gesoffen |
| saugen | to suck | saugt | sog, saugte | gesogen, gesaugt |
| schaffen | to create | schafft | schuf | geschaffen |
| scheiden | to separate | scheidet | schied | geschieden |
| scheinen | to shine, seem | scheint | schien | geschienen |
| scheißen | to shit | scheißt | schiss | geschissen |
| schelten | to scold | schilt | schalt | gescholten |
| scheren | to shear | schert | schor | geschoren |
| schieben | to push | schiebt | schob | geschoben |
| schießen | to shoot | schießt | schoss | geschossen |
| schinden | to maltreat | schindet | schindete | geschunden |
| schlafen | to sleep | schläft | schlief | geschlafen |
| schlagen | to beat, hit | schlägt | schlug | geschlagen |
| schleichen | to creep | schleicht | schlich | geschlichen* |
| schleifen | to sharpen | schleift | schliff | geschliffen |
| schließen | to shut | schließt | schloss | geschlossen |
| schlingen | to tie | schlingt | schlang | geschlungen |
| schmeißen | to chuck | schmeißt | schmiss | geschmissen |
| schmelzen | to melt | schmilzt | schmolz | geschmolzen |
| schneiden | to cut | schneidet | schnitt | geschnitten |
| schreiben | to write | schreibt | schrieb | geschrieben |
| schreien | to shout | schreit | schrie | geschrien |
| schreiten | to stride | schreitet | schritt | geschritten* |
| schweigen | to be silent | schweigt | schwieg | geschwiegen |
| schwellen | to swell | schwillt | schwoll | geschwollen* |
| schwimmen | to swim | schwimmt | schwamm | geschwommen* |

| | | | | |
|---|---|---|---|---|
| schwinden | to fade, dwindle | schwindet | schwand | geschwunden* |
| schwingen | to swing | schwingt | schwang | geschwungen |
| schwören | to swear | schwört | schwor | geschworen |
| sehen | to see | sieht | sah | gesehen; *(after infinitive)* sehen |
| sein | to be | ist | war | gewesen* |
| senden | to send | sendet | sandte | gesandt |
| singen | to sing | singt | sang | gesungen |
| sinken | to sink | sinkt | sank | gesunken* |
| sinnen | to ponder | sinnt | sann | gesonnen |
| sitzen | to sit | sitzt | saß | gesessen |
| sollen | to be supposed to | soll | sollte | gesollt; *(after infinitive)* sollen |
| spalten | to split | spaltet | spaltete | gespalten, gespaltet |
| speien | to spit, spew | speit | spie | gespien |
| spinnen | to spin | spinnt | spann | gesponnen |
| sprechen | to speak | spricht | sprach | gesprochen |
| sprießen | to sprout | sprießt | spross, sprießte | gesprossen* |
| springen | to jump | springt | sprang | gesprungen* |
| stechen | to sting | sticht | stach | gestochen |
| stecken | to be stuck | steckt | steckte, stak | gesteckt |
| stehen | to stand | steht | stand | gestanden |
| stehlen | to steal | stiehlt | stahl | gestohlen |
| steigen | to climb | steigt | stieg | gestiegen* |
| sterben | to die | stirbt | starb | gestorben* |
| stoßen | to push | stößt | stieß | gestoßen |
| streichen | to paint, spread, stroke, delete | streicht | strich | gestrichen |
| streiten | to argue | streitet | stritt | gestritten |
| tragen | to carry, wear | trägt | trug | getragen |
| treffen | to meet, hit | trifft | traf | getroffen |

| treiben | to drive, float | treibt | trieb | getrieben |
|---|---|---|---|---|
| treten | to kick, tread | tritt | trat | getreten |
| trinken | to drink | trinkt | trank | getrunken |
| trügen | to deceive | trügt | trog | getrogen |
| tun | to do | tut | tat | getan |
| verderben | to spoil | verdirbt | verdarb | verdorben |
| verdrießen | to annoy | verdrießt | verdross | verdrossen |
| vergessen | to forget | vergisst | vergaß | vergessen |
| verlieren | to lose | verliert | verlor | verloren |
| verschleißen | to wear out | verschleißt | verschliss | verschlissen |
| verzeihen | to forgive | verzeiht | verzieh | verziehen |
| wachsen | to grow | wächst | wuchs | gewachsen* |
| waschen | to wash | wäscht | wusch | gewaschen |
| weben | to weave | webt | webte, wob | gewebt, gewoben |
| weichen | to yield | weicht | wich | gewichen* |
| weisen | to show | weist | wies | gewiesen |
| wenden | to turn | wendet | wendete, wandte | gewendet, gewandt |
| werben | to advertise, recruit | wirbt | warb | geworben |
| werden | to become | wird | wurde | geworden*; *(after past participle)* worden |
| werfen | to throw | wirft | warf | geworfen |
| wiegen | to weigh | wiegt | wog | gewogen |
| winden | to wind | windet | wand | gewunden |
| winken | to wave | winkt | winkte | gewinkt, gewunken |
| wissen | to know | weiß | wusste | gewusst |
| wollen | to want to | will | wollte | gewollt; *(after infinitive)* wollen |
| wringen | to wring | wringt | wrang | gewrungen |
| ziehen | to pull | zieht | zog | gezogen |
| zwingen | to force | zwingt | zwang | gezwungen |

**D CONJUGATION TABLES**

The following verbs provide the main patterns of conjugation including the conjugation of some common irregular verbs. They are arranged in alphabetical order.

| | |
|---|---|
| Verbs with auxiliary **haben** (*see* pp 134-35) | BRAUCHEN |
| Verbs with auxiliary **sein** (*see* pp 135-36) | STÜRZEN |
| Reflexive verbs (*see* pp 165-67) | SICH BEEILEN |
| Separable verbs (*see* pp 139-40) | ABLEHNEN |
| Auxiliaries (*see* p 8) | HABEN |
| | SEIN |
| | WERDEN |
| Verbs with special endings (*see* p 114) | |
| Verbs ending in **-den/-ten/-men/-nen** | WARTEN |
| Verbs ending in **-ln/-rn** | ÄRGERN |
| Verbs ending in **-ssen** | PASSEN |
| Modal verbs (*see* pp 127-31, 157-62) | DÜRFEN |
| | KÖNNEN |
| | MÖGEN |
| | MÜSSEN |
| | SOLLEN |
| | WOLLEN |

'Chambers German Verbs', a fully comprehensive list of German verbs and their conjugations, is also available in this series.

# ABLEHNEN *to reject, decline*

| PRESENT | IMPERFECT | FUTURE |
|---|---|---|
| ich lehne ab | ich lehnte ab | ich werde ablehnen |
| du lehnst ab | du lehntest ab | du wirst ablehnen |
| er/sie lehnt ab | er/sie lehnte ab | er/sie wird ablehnen |
| wir lehnen ab | wir lehnten ab | wir werden ablehnen |
| ihr lehnt ab | ihr lehntet ab | ihr werdet ablehnen |
| Sie lehnen ab | Sie lehnten ab | Sie werden ablehnen |
| sie lehnen ab | sie lehnten ab | sie werden ablehnen |

| PERFECT | PLUPERFECT | CONDITIONAL |
|---|---|---|
| ich habe abgelehnt | ich hatte abgelehnt | ich würde ablehnen |
| du hast abgelehnt | du hattest abgelehnt | du würdest ablehnen |
| er/sie hat abgelehnt | er/sie hatte abgelehnt | er/sie würde ablehnen |
| wir haben abgelehnt | wir hatten abgelehnt | wir würden ablehnen |
| ihr habt abgelehnt | ihr hattet abgelehnt | ihr würdet ablehnen |
| Sie haben abgelehnt | Sie hatten abgelehnt | Sie würden ablehnen |
| sie haben abgelehnt | sie hatten abgelehnt | sie würden ablehnen |

## SUBJUNCTIVE

| PRESENT | PERFECT |
|---|---|
| ich lehne ab | ich habe abgelehnt |
| du lehnest ab | du habest abgelehnt |
| er/sie lehne ab | er/sie habe abgelehnt |
| wir lehnen ab | wir haben abgelehnt |
| ihr lehnet ab | ihr habet abgelehnt |
| Sie lehnen ab | Sie haben abgelehnt |
| sie lehnen ab | sie haben abgelehnt |

| IMPERFECT | PLUPERFECT |
|---|---|
| ich lehnte ab | ich hätte abgelehnt |
| du lehntest ab | du hättest abgelehnt |
| er/sie lehnte ab | er/sie hätte abgelehnt |
| wir lehnten ab | wir hätten abgelehnt |
| ihr lehntet ab | ihr hättet abgelehnt |
| Sie lehnten ab | Sie hätten abgelehnt |
| sie lehnten ab | sie hätten abgelehnt |

**FUTURE PERFECT**
ich werde abgelehnt haben
du wirst abgelehnt haben *etc*

## INFINITIVE

**PRESENT**
ablehnen
**PAST**
abgelehnt haben

## PARTICIPLE

**PRESENT**
ablehnend
**PAST**
abgelehnt

## IMPERATIVE

lehn(e) ab!
lehnt ab!
lehnen Sie ab!
lehnen wir ab!

# ÄRGERN *to annoy*

| **PRESENT** | **IMPERFECT** | **FUTURE** |
|---|---|---|
| ich ärgere | ich ärgerte | ich werde ärgern |
| du ärgerst | du ärgertest | du wirst ärgern |
| er/sie ärgert | er/sie ärgerte | er/sie wird ärgern |
| wir ärgern | wir ärgerten | wir werden ärgern |
| ihr ärgert | ihr ärgertet | ihr werdet ärgern |
| Sie ärgern | Sie ärgerten | Sie werden ärgern |
| sie ärgern | sie ärgerten | sie werden ärgern |

| **PERFECT** | **PLUPERFECT** | **CONDITIONAL** |
|---|---|---|
| ich habe geärgert | ich hatte geärgert | ich würde ärgern |
| du hast geärgert | du hattest geärgert | du würdest ärgern |
| er/sie hat geärgert | er/sie hatte geärgert | er/sie würde ärgern |
| wir haben geärgert | wir hatten geärgert | wir würden ärgern |
| ihr habt geärgert | ihr hattet geärgert | ihr würdet ärgern |
| Sie haben geärgert | Sie hatten geärgert | Sie würden ärgern |
| sie haben geärgert | sie hatten geärgert | sie würden ärgern |

## *SUBJUNCTIVE*

| **PRESENT** | **PERFECT** |
|---|---|
| ich ärgere | ich habe geärgert |
| du ärgerest | du habest geärgert |
| er/sie ärgere | er/sie habe geärgert |
| wir ärgeren | wir haben geärgert |
| ihr ärgeret | ihr habet geärgert |
| Sie ärgeren | Sie haben geärgert |
| sie ärgeren | sie haben geärgert |

| **IMPERFECT** | **PLUPERFECT** |
|---|---|
| ich ärgerte | ich hätte geärgert |
| du ärgertest | du hättest geärgert |
| er/sie ärgerte | er/sie hätte geärgert |
| wir ärgerten | wir hätten geärgert |
| ihr ärgertet | ihr hättet geärgert |
| Sie ärgerten | Sie hätten geärgert |
| sie ärgerten | sie hätten geärgert |

**FUTURE PERFECT**
ich werde geärgert haben
du wirst geärgert haben *etc*

## *INFINITIVE*

**PRESENT**
ärgern
**PAST**
geärgert haben

## *PARTICIPLE*

**PRESENT**
ärgernd
**PAST**
geärgert

## *IMPERATIVE*

ärg(e)re!
ärgert!
ärgern Sie!
ärgern wir!

# SICH BEEILEN *to hurry, rush*

**PRESENT**
ich beeile mich
du beeilst dich
er/sie beeilt sich
wir beeilen uns
ihr beeilt euch
Sie beeilen sich
sie beeilen sich

**IMPERFECT**
ich beeilte mich
du beeiltest dich
er/sie beeilte sich
wir beeilten uns
ihr beeiltet euch
Sie beeilten sich
sie beeilten sich

**FUTURE**
ich werde mich beeilen
du wirst dich beeilen
er/sie wird sich beeilen
wir werden uns beeilen
ihr werdet euch beeilen
Sie werden sich beeilen
sie werden sich beeilen

**PERFECT**
ich habe mich beeilt
du hast dich beeilt
er/sie hat sich beeilt
wir haben uns beeilt
ihr habt euch beeilt
Sie haben sich beeilt
sie haben sich beeilt

**PLUPERFECT**
ich hatte mich beeilt
du hattest dich beeilt
er/sie hatte sich beeilt
wir hatten uns beeilt
ihr hattet euch beeilt
Sie hatten sich beeilt
sie hatten sich beeilt

**CONDITIONAL**
ich würde mich beeilen
du würdest dich beeilen
er/sie würde sich beeilen
wir würden uns beeilen
ihr würdet euch beeilen
Sie würden sich beeilen
sie würden sich beeilen

## SUBJUNCTIVE

**PRESENT**
ich beeile mich
du beeilest dich
er/sie beeile sich
wir beeilen uns
ihr beeilet euch
Sie beeilen sich
sie beeilen sich

**IMPERFECT**
ich beeilte mich
du beeiltest dich
er/sie beeilte sich
wir beeilten uns
ihr beeiltet euch
Sie beeilten sich
sie beeilten sich

**FUTURE PERFECT**
ich werde mich beeilt haben
du wirst dich beeilt haben *etc*

**PERFECT**
ich habe mich beeilt
du habest dich beeilt
er/sie habe sich beeilt
wir haben uns beeilt
ihr habet euch beeilt
Sie haben sich beeilt
sie haben sich beeilt

**PLUPERFECT**
ich hätte mich beeilt
du hättest dich beeilt
er/sie hätte sich beeilt
wir hätten uns beeilt
ihr hättet euch beeilt
Sie hätten sich beeilt
sie hätten sich beeilt

## INFINITIVE

**PRESENT**
sich beeilen
**PAST**
sich beeilt haben

## PARTICIPLE

**PRESENT**
mich/sich *etc* beeilend

## IMPERATIVE

beeile dich!
beeilt euch!
beeilen Sie sich!
beeilen wir uns!

# BRAUCHEN *to need*

**PRESENT**
ich brauche
du brauchst
er/sie braucht
wir brauchen
ihr braucht
Sie brauchen
sie brauchen

**PERFECT**
ich habe gebraucht
du hast gebraucht
er/sie hat gebraucht
wir haben gebraucht
ihr habt gebraucht
Sie haben gebraucht
sie haben gebraucht

**IMPERFECT**
ich brauchte
du brauchtest
er/sie brauchte
wir brauchten
ihr brauchtet
Sie brauchten
sie brauchten

**PLUPERFECT**
ich hatte gebraucht
du hattest gebraucht
er/sie hatte gebraucht
wir hatten gebraucht
ihr hattet gebraucht
Sie hatten gebraucht
sie hatten gebraucht

**FUTURE**
ich werde brauchen
du wirst brauchen
er/sie wird brauchen
wir werden brauchen
ihr werdet brauchen
Sie werden brauchen
sie werden brauchen

**CONDITIONAL**
ich würde brauchen
du würdest brauchen
er/sie würde brauchen
wir würden brauchen
ihr würdet brauchen
Sie würden brauchen
sie würden brauchen

## SUBJUNCTIVE

**PRESENT**
ich brauche
du brauchest
er/sie brauche
wir brauchen
ihr brauchet
Sie brauchen
sie brauchen

**IMPERFECT**
ich brauchte
du brauchtest
er/sie brauchte
wir brauchten
ihr brauchtet
Sie brauchten
sie brauchten

**FUTURE PERFECT**
ich werde gebraucht haben
du wirst gebraucht haben *etc*

**PERFECT**
ich habe gebraucht
du habest gebraucht
er/sie habe gebraucht
wir haben gebraucht
ihr habet gebraucht
Sie haben gebraucht
sie haben gebraucht

**PLUPERFECT**
ich hätte gebraucht
du hättest gebraucht
er/sie hätte gebraucht
wir hätten gebraucht
ihr hättet gebraucht
Sie hätten gebraucht
sie hätten gebraucht

## INFINITIVE

**PRESENT**
brauchen
**PAST**
gebraucht haben

## PARTICIPLE

**PRESENT**
brauchend
**PAST**
gebraucht

## IMPERATIVE

brauch(e)!
braucht!
brauchen Sie!
brauchen wir!

# DÜRFEN *to be allowed to*

**PRESENT**
ich darf
du darfst
er/sie darf
wir dürfen
ihr dürft
Sie dürfen
sie dürfen

**PERFECT** *(1)*
ich habe gedurft
du hast gedurft
er/sie hat gedurft
wir haben gedurft
ihr habt gedurft
Sie haben gedurft
sie haben gedurft

**IMPERFECT**
ich durfte
du durftest
er/sie durfte
wir durften
ihr durftet
Sie durften
sie durften

**PLUPERFECT** *(2)*
ich hatte gedurft
du hattest gedurft
er/sie hatte gedurft
wir hatten gedurft
ihr hattet gedurft
Sie hatten gedurft
sie hatten gedurft

**FUTURE**
ich werde dürfen
du wirst dürfen
er/sie wird dürfen
wir werden dürfen
ihr werdet dürfen
Sie werden dürfen
sie werden dürfen

**CONDITIONAL**
ich würde dürfen
du würdest dürfen
er/sie würde dürfen
wir würden dürfen
ihr würdet dürfen
Sie würden dürfen
sie würden dürfen

## SUBJUNCTIVE

**PRESENT**
ich dürfe
du dürfest
er/sie dürfe
wir dürfen
ihr dürfet
Sie dürfen
sie dürfen

**IMPERFECT**
ich dürfte
du dürftest
er/sie dürfte
wir dürften
ihr dürftet
Sie dürften
sie dürften

**PERFECT** *(1)*
ich habe gedurft
du habest gedurft
er/sie habe gedurft
wir haben gedurft
ihr habet gedurft
Sie haben gedurft
sie haben gedurft

**PLUPERFECT** *(3)*
ich hätte gedurft
du hättest gedurft
er/sie hätte gedurft
wir hätten gedurft
ihr hättet gedurft
Sie hätten gedurft
sie hätten gedurft

## INFINITIVE

**PRESENT**
dürfen
**PAST**
gedurft haben

## PARTICIPLE

**PRESENT**
dürfend
**PAST**
gedurft

**NOTE** *when preceded by an infinitive: (1)* ich habe ... dürfen *etc (2)* ich hatte ... dürfen *etc (3)* ich hätte ... dürfen *etc*

# HABEN *to have*

| PRESENT | IMPERFECT | FUTURE |
|---|---|---|
| ich habe | ich hatte | ich werde haben |
| du hast | du hattest | du wirst haben |
| er/sie hat | er/sie hatte | er/sie wird haben |
| wir haben | wir hatten | wir werden haben |
| ihr habt | ihr hattet | ihr werdet haben |
| Sie haben | Sie hatten | Sie werden haben |
| sie haben | sie hatten | sie werden haben |
| **PERFECT** | **PLUPERFECT** | **CONDITIONAL** |
| ich habe gehabt | ich hatte gehabt | ich würde haben |
| du hast gehabt | du hattest gehabt | du würdest haben |
| er/sie hat gehabt | er/sie hatte gehabt | er/sie würde haben |
| wir haben gehabt | wir hatten gehabt | wir würden haben |
| ihr habt gehabt | ihr hattet gehabt | ihr würdet haben |
| Sie haben gehabt | Sie hatten gehabt | Sie würden haben |
| sie haben gehabt | sie hatten gehabt | sie würden haben |

## *SUBJUNCTIVE*

| PRESENT | PERFECT |
|---|---|
| ich habe | ich habe gehabt |
| du habest | du habest gehabt |
| er/sie habe | er/sie habe gehabt |
| wir haben | wir haben gehabt |
| ihr habet | ihr habet gehabt |
| Sie haben | Sie haben gehabt |
| sie haben | sie haben gehabt |
| **IMPERFECT** | **PLUPERFECT** |
| ich hätte | ich hätte gehabt |
| du hättest | du hättest gehabt |
| er/sie hätte | er/sie hätte gehabt |
| wir hätten | wir hätten gehabt |
| ihr hättet | ihr hättet gehabt |
| Sie hätten | Sie hätten gehabt |
| sie hätten | sie hätten gehabt |

**FUTURE PERFECT**
ich werde gehabt haben
du wirst gehabt haben *etc*

## *INFINITIVE*

**PRESENT**
haben
**PAST**
gehabt haben

## *PARTICIPLE*

**PRESENT**
habend
**PAST**
gehabt

## *IMPERATIVE*

hab(e)!
habt!
haben Sie!
haben wir!

# KÖNNEN *to be able to*

| **PRESENT** | **IMPERFECT** | **FUTURE** |
|---|---|---|
| ich kann | ich konnte | ich werde können |
| du kannst | du konntest | du wirst können |
| er/sie kann | er/sie konnte | er/sie wird können |
| wir können | wir konnten | wir werden können |
| ihr könnt | ihr konntet | ihr werdet können |
| Sie können | Sie konnten | Sie werden können |
| sie können | sie konnten | sie werden können |
| **PERFECT** *(1)* | **PLUPERFECT** *(2)* | **CONDITIONAL** |
| ich habe gekonnt | ich hatte gekonnt | ich würde können |
| du hast gekonnt | du hattest gekonnt | du würdest können |
| er/sie hat gekonnt | er/sie hatte gekonnt | er/sie würde können |
| wir haben gekonnt | wir hatten gekonnt | wir würden können |
| ihr habt gekonnt | ihr hattet gekonnt | ihr würdet können |
| Sie haben gekonnt | Sie hatten gekonnt | Sie würden können |
| sie haben gekonnt | sie hatten gekonnt | sie würden können |

## *SUBJUNCTIVE*

| **PRESENT** | **PERFECT** *(1)* |
|---|---|
| ich könne | ich habe gekonnt |
| du könnest | du habest gekonnt |
| er/sie könne | er/sie habe gekonnt |
| wir können | wir haben gekonnt |
| ihr könnet | ihr habet gekonnt |
| Sie können | Sie haben gekonnt |
| sie können | sie haben gekonnt |
| **IMPERFECT** | **PLUPERFECT** *(3)* |
| ich könnte | ich hätte gekonnt |
| du könntest | du hättest gekonnt |
| er/sie könnte | er/sie hätte gekonnt |
| wir könnten | wir hätten gekonnt |
| ihr könntet | ihr hättet gekonnt |
| Sie könnten | Sie hätten gekonnt |
| sie könnten | sie hätten gekonnt |

## *INFINITIVE*

**PRESENT**
können

**PAST**
gekonnt haben

## *PARTICIPLE*

**PRESENT**
könnend

**PAST**
gekonnt

*NOTE when preceded by an infinitive: (1)* ich habe ... können *etc (2)* ich hatte ... können *etc (3)* ich hätte ... können *etc*

# MÖGEN *to like*

| PRESENT | IMPERFECT | FUTURE |
|---|---|---|
| ich mag | ich mochte | ich werde mögen |
| du magst | du mochtest | du wirst mögen |
| er/sie mag | er/sie mochte | er/sie wird mögen |
| wir mögen | wir mochten | wir werden mögen |
| ihr mögt | ihr mochtet | ihr werdet mögen |
| Sie mögen | Sie mochten | Sie werden mögen |
| sie mögen | sie mochten | sie werden mögen |

| PERFECT *(1)* | PLUPERFECT *(2)* | CONDITIONAL |
|---|---|---|
| ich habe gemocht | ich hatte gemocht | ich würde mögen |
| du hast gemocht | du hattest gemocht | du würdest mögen |
| er/sie hat gemocht | er/sie hatte gemocht | er/sie würde mögen |
| wir haben gemocht | wir hatten gemocht | wir würden mögen |
| ihr habt gemocht | ihr hattet gemocht | ihr würdet mögen |
| Sie haben gemocht | Sie hatten gemocht | Sie würden mögen |
| sie haben gemocht | sie hatten gemocht | sie würden mögen |

## SUBJUNCTIVE

| PRESENT | PERFECT *(1)* |
|---|---|
| ich möge | ich habe gemocht |
| du mögest | du habest gemocht |
| er/sie möge | er/sie habe gemocht |
| wir mögen | wir haben gemocht |
| ihr möget | ihr habet gemocht |
| Sie mögen | Sie haben gemocht |
| sie mögen | sie haben gemocht |

| IMPERFECT | PLUPERFECT *(3)* |
|---|---|
| ich möchte | ich hätte gemocht |
| du möchtest | du hättest gemocht |
| er/sie möchte | er/sie hätte gemocht |
| wir möchten | wir hätten gemocht |
| ihr möchtet | ihr hättet gemocht |
| Sie möchten | Sie hätten gemocht |
| sie möchten | sie hätten gemocht |

## INFINITIVE

**PRESENT**
mögen

**PAST**
gemocht haben

## PARTICIPLE

**PRESENT**
mögend

**PAST**
gemocht

**NOTE** when preceded by an infinitive: *(1)* ich habe ... mögen *etc (2)* ich hatte ... mögen *etc (3)* ich hätte ... mögen *etc*

# MÜSSEN *to have to*

| PRESENT | IMPERFECT | FUTURE |
|---|---|---|
| ich muss | ich musste | ich werde müssen |
| du musst | du musstest | du wirst müssen |
| er/sie muss | er/sie musste | er/sie wird müssen |
| wir müssen | wir mussten | wir werden müssen |
| ihr müsst | ihr musstet | ihr werdet müssen |
| Sie müssen | Sie mussten | Sie werden müssen |
| sie müssen | sie mussten | sie werden müssen |
| **PERFECT** *(1)* | **PLUPERFECT** *(2)* | **CONDITIONAL** |
| ich habe gemusst | ich hatte gemusst | ich würde müssen |
| du hast gemusst | du hattest gemusst | du würdest müssen |
| er/sie hat gemusst | er/sie hatte gemusst | er/sie würde müssen |
| wir haben gemusst | wir hatten gemusst | wir würden müssen |
| ihr habt gemusst | ihr hattet gemusst | ihr würdet müssen |
| Sie haben gemusst | Sie hatten gemusst | Sie würden müssen |
| sie haben gemusst | sie hatten gemusst | sie würden müssen |

## *SUBJUNCTIVE*

## *INFINITIVE*

| PRESENT | PERFECT *(1)* | PRESENT |
|---|---|---|
| ich müsse | ich habe gemusst | müssen |
| du müssest | du habest gemusst | **PAST** |
| er/sie müsse | er/sie habe gemusst | gemusst haben |
| wir müssen | wir haben gemusst | |
| ihr müsset | ihr habet gemusst | *PARTICIPLE* |
| Sie müssen | Sie haben gemusst | |
| sie müssen | sie haben gemusst | PRESENT |
| **IMPERFECT** | **PLUPERFECT** *(3)* | müssend |
| ich müsste | ich hätte gemusst | **PAST** |
| du müsstest | du hättest gemusst | gemusst |
| er/sie müsste | er/sie hätte gemusst | |
| wir müssten | wir hätten gemusst | |
| ihr müsstet | ihr hättet gemusst | |
| Sie müssten | Sie hätten gemusst | |
| sie müssten | sie hätten gemusst | |

***NOTE** when preceded by an infinitive: (1) ich habe ... müssen etc (2) ich hatte ... müssen etc (3) ich hätte ... müssen etc*

# PASSEN *to fit, suit*

| PRESENT | IMPERFECT | FUTURE |
|---|---|---|
| ich passe | ich passte | ich werde passen |
| du passt | du passtest | du wirst passen |
| er/sie passt | er/sie passte | er/sie wird passen |
| wir passen | wir passten | wir werden passen |
| ihr passt | ihr passtet | ihr werdet passen |
| Sie passen | Sie passten | Sie werden passen |
| sie passen | sie passten | sie werden passen |

| PERFECT | PLUPERFECT | CONDITIONAL |
|---|---|---|
| ich habe gepasst | ich hatte gepasst | ich würde passen |
| du hast gepasst | du hattest gepasst | du würdest passen |
| er/sie hat gepasst | er/sie hatte gepasst | er/sie würde passen |
| wir haben gepasst | wir hatten gepasst | wir würden passen |
| ihr habt gepasst | ihr hattet gepasst | ihr würdet passen |
| Sie haben gepasst | Sie hatten gepasst | Sie würden passen |
| sie haben gepasst | sie hatten gepasst | sie würden passen |

## SUBJUNCTIVE

| PRESENT | PERFECT |
|---|---|
| ich passe | ich habe gepasst |
| du passest | du habest gepasst |
| er/sie passe | er/sie habe gepasst |
| wir passen | wir haben gepasst |
| ihr passet | ihr habet gepasst |
| Sie passen | Sie haben gepasst |
| sie passen | sie haben gepasst |

| IMPERFECT | PLUPERFECT |
|---|---|
| ich passte | ich hätte gepasst |
| du passtest | du hättest gepasst |
| er/sie passte | er/sie hätte gepasst |
| wir passten | wir hätten gepasst |
| ihr passtet | ihr hättet gepasst |
| Sie passten | Sie hätten gepasst |
| sie passten | sie hätten gepasst |

FUTURE PERFECT
ich werde gepasst haben
du wirst gepasst haben *etc*

## INFINITIVE

PRESENT
passen
PAST
gepasst haben

## PARTICIPLE

PRESENT
passend
PAST
gepasst

## IMPERATIVE

pass! passe!
passt!
passen Sie!
passen wir!

# SEIN *to be*

| PRESENT | IMPERFECT | FUTURE |
|---|---|---|
| ich bin | ich war | ich werde sein |
| du bist | du warst | du wirst sein |
| er/sie ist | er/sie war | er/sie wird sein |
| wir sind | wir waren | wir werden sein |
| ihr seid | ihr wart | ihr werdet sein |
| Sie sind | Sie waren | Sie werden sein |
| sie sind | sie waren | sie werden sein |

| PERFECT | PLUPERFECT | CONDITIONAL |
|---|---|---|
| ich bin gewesen | ich war gewesen | ich würde sein |
| du bist gewesen | du warst gewesen | du würdest sein |
| er/sie ist gewesen | er/sie war gewesen | er/sie würde sein |
| wir sind gewesen | wir waren gewesen | wir würden sein |
| ihr seid gewesen | ihr wart gewesen | ihr würdet sein |
| Sie sind gewesen | Sie waren gewesen | Sie würden sein |
| sie sind gewesen | sie waren gewesen | sie würden sein |

## SUBJUNCTIVE

| PRESENT | PERFECT |
|---|---|
| ich sei | ich sei gewesen |
| du sei(e)st | du sei(e)st gewesen |
| er/sie sei | er/sie sei gewesen |
| wir seien | wir seien gewesen |
| ihr seiet | ihr seiet gewesen |
| Sie seien | Sie seien gewesen |
| sie seien | sie seien gewesen |

| IMPERFECT | PLUPERFECT |
|---|---|
| ich wäre | ich wäre gewesen |
| du wär(e)st | du wär(e)st gewesen |
| er/sie wäre | er/sie wäre gewesen |
| wir wären | wir wären gewesen |
| ihr wär(e)t | ihr wär(e)t gewesen |
| Sie wären | Sie wären gewesen |
| sie wären | sie wären gewesen |

FUTURE PERFECT
ich werde gewesen sein
du wirst gewesen sein *etc*

## INFINITIVE

PRESENT
sein
PAST
gewesen sein

## PARTICIPLE

PRESENT
seiend
PAST
gewesen

## IMPERATIVE

sei!
seid!
seien Sie!
seien wir!

# SOLLEN  *to be supposed to*

| PRESENT | IMPERFECT | FUTURE |
|---|---|---|
| ich soll | ich sollte | ich werde sollen |
| du sollst | du solltest | du wirst sollen |
| er/sie soll | er/sie sollte | er/sie wird sollen |
| wir sollen | wir sollten | wir werden sollen |
| ihr sollt | ihr solltet | ihr werdet sollen |
| Sie sollen | Sie sollten | Sie werden sollen |
| sie sollen | sie sollten | sie werden sollen |
| PERFECT *(1)* | PLUPERFECT *(2)* | CONDITIONAL |
| ich habe gesollt | ich hatte gesollt | ich würde sollen |
| du hast gesollt | du hattest gesollt | du würdest sollen |
| er/sie hat gesollt | er/sie hatte gesollt | er/sie würde sollen |
| wir haben gesollt | wir hatten gesollt | wir würden sollen |
| ihr habt gesollt | ihr hattet gesollt | ihr würdet sollen |
| Sie haben gesollt | Sie hatten gesollt | Sie würden sollen |
| sie haben gesollt | sie hatten gesollt | sie würden sollen |

## SUBJUNCTIVE

## INFINITIVE

| PRESENT | PERFECT *(1)* |
|---|---|
| ich solle | ich habe gesollt |
| du sollest | du habest gesollt |
| er/sie solle | er/sie habe gesollt |
| wir sollen | wir haben gesollt |
| ihr sollet | ihr habet gesollt |
| Sie sollen | Sie haben gesollt |
| sie sollen | sie haben gesollt |

PRESENT
sollen
PAST
gesollt haben

## PARTICIPLE

PRESENT
sollend
PAST
gesollt

| IMPERFECT | PLUPERFECT *(3)* |
|---|---|
| ich sollte | ich hätte gesollt |
| du solltest | du hättest gesollt |
| er/sie sollte | er/sie hätte gesollt |
| wir sollten | wir hätten gesollt |
| ihr solltet | ihr hättet gesollt |
| Sie sollten | Sie hätten gesollt |
| sie sollten | sie hätten gesollt |

*NOTE when preceded by an infinitive: (1) ich habe ... sollen etc (2) ich hatte ... sollen etc (3) ich hätte ... sollen etc*

# STÜRZEN *to fall, plunge, rush*

| **PRESENT** | **IMPERFECT** | **FUTURE** |
|---|---|---|
| ich stürze | ich stürzte | ich werde stürzen |
| du stürzt | du stürztest | du wirst stürzen |
| er/sie stürzt | er/sie stürzte | er/sie wird stürzen |
| wir stürzen | wir stürzten | wir werden stürzen |
| ihr stürzt | ihr stürztet | ihr werdet stürzen |
| Sie stürzen | Sie stürzten | Sie werden stürzen |
| sie stürzen | sie stürzten | sie werden stürzen |

| **PERFECT** | **PLUPERFECT** | **CONDITIONAL** |
|---|---|---|
| ich bin gestürzt | ich war gestürzt | ich würde stürzen |
| du bist gestürzt | du warst gestürzt | du würdest stürzen |
| er/sie ist gestürzt | er/sie war gestürzt | er/sie würde stürzen |
| wir sind gestürzt | wir waren gestürzt | wir würden stürzen |
| ihr seid gestürzt | ihr wart gestürzt | ihr würdet stürzen |
| Sie sind gestürzt | Sie waren gestürzt | Sie würden stürzen |
| sie sind gestürzt | sie waren gestürzt | sie würden stürzen |

## *SUBJUNCTIVE*

| **PRESENT** | **PERFECT** |
|---|---|
| ich stürze | ich sei gestürzt |
| du stürzest | du sei(e)st gestürzt |
| er/sie stürze | er/sie sei gestürzt |
| wir stürzen | wir seien gestürzt |
| ihr stürzet | ihr seiet gestürzt |
| Sie stürzen | Sie seien gestürzt |
| sie stürzen | sie seien gestürzt |

| **IMPERFECT** | **PLUPERFECT** |
|---|---|
| ich stürzte | ich wäre gestürzt |
| du stürztest | du wär(e)st gestürzt |
| er/sie stürzte | er/sie wäre gestürzt |
| wir stürzten | wir wären gestürzt |
| ihr stürztet | ihr wär(e)t gestürzt |
| Sie stürzten | Sie wären gestürzt |
| sie stürzten | sie wären gestürzt |

**FUTURE PERFECT**
ich werde gestürzt sein
du wirst gestürzt sein *etc*

## *INFINITIVE*

**PRESENT**
stürzen
**PAST**
gestürzt sein

## *PARTICIPLE*

**PRESENT**
stürzend
**PAST**
gestürzt

## *IMPERATIVE*

stürz(e)!
stürzt!
stürzen Sie!
stürzen wir!

# WARTEN *to wait*

| PRESENT | IMPERFECT | FUTURE |
|---|---|---|
| ich warte | ich wartete | ich werde warten |
| du wartest | du wartetest | du wirst warten |
| er/sie wartet | er/sie wartete | er/sie wird warten |
| wir warten | wir warteten | wir werden warten |
| ihr wartet | ihr wartetet | ihr werdet warten |
| Sie warten | Sie warteten | Sie werden warten |
| sie warten | sie warteten | sie werden warten |

| PERFECT | PLUPERFECT | CONDITIONAL |
|---|---|---|
| ich habe gewartet | ich hatte gewartet | ich würde warten |
| du hast gewartet | du hattest gewartet | du würdest warten |
| er/sie hat gewartet | er/sie hatte gewartet | er/sie würde warten |
| wir haben gewartet | wir hatten gewartet | wir würden warten |
| ihr habt gewartet | ihr hattet gewartet | ihr würdet warten |
| Sie haben gewartet | Sie hatten gewartet | Sie würden warten |
| sie haben gewartet | sie hatten gewartet | sie würden warten |

## *SUBJUNCTIVE*

| PRESENT | PERFECT |
|---|---|
| ich warte | ich habe gewartet |
| du wartest | du habest gewartet |
| er/sie warte | er/sie habe gewartet |
| wir warten | wir haben gewartet |
| ihr wartet | ihr habet gewartet |
| Sie warten | Sie haben gewartet |
| sie warten | sie haben gewartet |

| IMPERFECT | PLUPERFECT |
|---|---|
| ich wartete | ich hätte gewartet |
| du wartetest | du hättest gewartet |
| er/sie wartete | er/sie hätte gewartet |
| wir warteten | wir hätten gewartet |
| ihr wartetet | ihr hättet gewartet |
| Sie warteten | Sie hätten gewartet |
| sie warteten | sie hätten gewartet |

**FUTURE PERFECT**
ich werde gewartet haben
du wirst gewartet haben *etc*

## *INFINITIVE*

**PRESENT**
warten

**PAST**
gewartet haben

## *PARTICIPLE*

**PRESENT**
wartend

**PAST**
gewartet

## *IMPERATIVE*

warte(e)!
wartet!
warten Sie!
warten wir!

# WERDEN *to become*

| **PRESENT** | **IMPERFECT** | **FUTURE** |
|---|---|---|
| ich werde | ich wurde | ich werde werden |
| du wirst | du wurdest | du wirst werden |
| er/sie wird | er/sie wurde | er/sie wird werden |
| wir werden | wir wurden | wir werden werden |
| ihr werdet | ihr wurdet | ihr werdet werden |
| Sie werden | Sie wurden | Sie werden werden |
| sie werden | sie wurden | sie werden werden |

| **PERFECT** *(1)* | **PLUPERFECT** *(2)* | **CONDITIONAL** |
|---|---|---|
| ich bin geworden | ich war geworden | ich würde werden |
| du bist geworden | du warst geworden | du würdest werden |
| er/sie ist geworden | er/sie war geworden | er/sie würde werden |
| wir sind geworden | wir waren geworden | wir würden werden |
| ihr seid geworden | ihr wart geworden | ihr würdet werden |
| Sie sind geworden | Sie waren geworden | Sie würden werden |
| sie sind geworden | sie waren geworden | sie würden werden |

## SUBJUNCTIVE

| **PRESENT** | **PERFECT** *(3)* |
|---|---|
| ich werde | ich sei geworden |
| du werdest | du sei(e)st geworden |
| er/sie werde | er/sie sei geworden |
| wir werden | wir seien geworden |
| ihr werdet | ihr seiet geworden |
| Sie werden | Sie seien geworden |
| sie werden | sie seien geworden |

| **IMPERFECT** | **PLUPERFECT** *(4)* |
|---|---|
| ich würde | ich wäre geworden |
| du würdest | du wär(e)st geworden |
| er/sie würde | er/sie wäre geworden |
| wir würden | wir wären geworden |
| ihr würdet | ihr wär(e)t geworden |
| Sie würden | Sie wären geworden |
| sie würden | sie wären geworden |

| **FUTURE PERFECT** *(5)* |
|---|
| ich werde geworden sein |
| du wirst geworden |
| sein *etc* |

## INFINITIVE

**PRESENT**
werden

**PAST** *(6)*
geworden sein

## PARTICIPLE

**PRESENT**
werdend

**PAST**
geworden

## IMPERATIVE

werde!
werdet!
werden Sie!
werden wir!

**NOTE** geworden *becomes* worden *when preceded by a past participle to form the passive :* (1) ich bin ... worden *etc* (2) ich war ...worden *etc* (3) ich sei ... worden *etc* (4) ich wäre ...worden *etc* (5) ich werde ... worden sein *etc* (6) ...worden sein

# WOLLEN *to want (to)*

| PRESENT | IMPERFECT | FUTURE |
|---|---|---|
| ich will | ich wollte | ich werde wollen |
| du willst | du wolltest | du wirst wollen |
| er/sie will | er/sie wollte | er/sie wird wollen |
| wir wollen | wir wollten | wir werden wollen |
| ihr wollt | ihr wolltet | ihr werdet wollen |
| Sie wollen | Sie wollten | Sie werden wollen |
| sie wollen | sie wollten | sie werden wollen |

| PERFECT *(1)* | PLUPERFECT *(2)* | CONDITIONAL |
|---|---|---|
| ich habe gewollt | ich hatte gewollt | ich würde wollen |
| du hast gewollt | du hattest gewollt | du würdest wollen |
| er/sie hat gewollt | er/sie hatte gewollt | er/sie würde wollen |
| wir haben gewollt | wir hatten gewollt | wir würden wollen |
| ihr habt gewollt | ihr hattet gewollt | ihr würdet wollen |
| Sie haben gewollt | Sie hatten gewollt | Sie würden wollen |
| sie haben gewollt | sie hatten gewollt | sie würden wollen |

## *SUBJUNCTIVE*

### *INFINITIVE*

| PRESENT | PERFECT *(1)* |
|---|---|
| ich wolle | ich habe gewollt |
| du wollest | du habest gewollt |
| er/sie wolle | er/sie habe gewollt |
| wir wollen | wir haben gewollt |
| ihr wollet | ihr habet gewollt |
| Sie wollen | Sie haben gewollt |
| sie wollen | sie haben gewollt |

**PRESENT**
wollen
**PAST**
gewollt haben

### *PARTICIPLE*

| IMPERFECT | PLUPERFECT *(3)* |
|---|---|
| ich wollte | ich hätte gewollt |
| du wolltest | du hättest gewollt |
| er/sie wollte | er/sie hätte gewollt |
| wir wollten | wir hätten gewollt |
| ihr wolltet | ihr hättet gewollt |
| Sie wollten | Sie hätten gewollt |
| sie wollten | sie hätten gewollt |

**PRESENT**
wollend
**PAST**
gewollt

### *IMPERATIVE*

woll(e)!
wollt!
wollen Sie!
wollen wir!

**NOTE:** *when preceded by an infinitive: (1)* ich habe ... wollen *etc (2)* ich hatte ... wollen *etc (3)* ich hätte ... wollen *etc*

# 8 PREPOSITIONS

Prepositions are words such as 'from', 'in', 'with'. They are followed by nouns or pronouns, which, in German, must be in the case determined by the preposition. Many take only one case, but some are followed by one of two cases (*see* sections C and E).

The most common prepositions are given below in five categories according to whether they take the dative, the accusative, the genitive, the dative or accusative, or the genitive or dative case. They are listed in alphabetical order, with the generally accepted meanings on the left, a description of their use in brackets, and an illustration of their usage.

## A WITH THE DATIVE ONLY

**AUS**

| OUT OF | *(place)* | **er lief aus dem Haus**<br>he ran out of the house |
|---|---|---|
| FROM | *(place)* | **ich stamme aus Italien**<br>I come from Italy |
| | *(place)* | **aus dieser Richtung**<br>from this direction |
| | *(time)* | **ein Gemälde aus dem 18. Jahrhundert**<br>a painting from the 18th century |
| | *(cause)* | **aus Langeweile**<br>from boredom |
| MADE OF | *(material)* | **aus Messing**<br>made of brass |

**AUSSER**

| APART FROM | | **außer einem Frosch habe ich keine Haustiere**<br>apart from a frog I don't have any pets |
|---|---|---|

| OUT OF | | **außer Atem/Betrieb/Gefahr/Kontrolle** |
| | | out of breath/order/danger/control |
| OUT | *(idiom)* | **wir essen nie außer Hause** |
| | | we never eat out |

**BEI**

| NEAR | *(place)* | **er wohnt bei der Post** |
| | | he lives near the post |
| AT | *(place)* | **bei mir/Ihnen/Schmidts** |
| | | at my/your/the Schmidts' house |
| | | **beim Bäcker** |
| | | at the baker's |
| | | **bei Woolworth** |
| | | at Woolworth's |
| | *(time)* | **bei Tagesanbruch** |
| | | at daybreak |

Note that bei cannot be used with verbs of motion:

**er übernachtet bei seiner Mutter**
he's spending the night at his mother's

*but:*

**er fährt gerade zu seiner Mutter**
he's on his way to his mother's

| ON | *(time)* | **bei seiner Ankunft/Abfahrt** |
| | | on his arrival/departure |
| | *(position)* | **hat jemand Geld bei sich?** |
| | | has anyone got any money on them? |
| WITH | *(+ pronoun)* | **bei ihr war es anders** |
| | | with her it was different |
| IN | *(with writers etc)* | **bei Goethe/Shakespeare** |
| | | in Goethe/Shakespeare |
| BY | *(time)* | **bei Tag/Nacht** |
| | | by day/night |
| — | *(+ gerund)* | **er ist gerade beim Abwaschen** |
| | | he's (just) washing up |

## PREPOSITIONS

### GEGENÜBER

| OPPOSITE/ FACING | *(place)* | **gegenüber dem Park/dem Park gegenüber** |
| | | opposite the park |
| TOWARDS | *(relationship)* | **er ist mir gegenüber sehr freundlich** |
| | | he's very friendly towards me |
| COMPARED WITH | | **ihm gegenüber ist sie fast ein Genie** |
| | | compared with him she's practically a genius |

### GEMÄSS

| IN ACCORDANCE WITH | **unseren Wünschen gemäß** |
| | in accordance with our wishes |

### MIT

| WITH | *(association)* | **mit nur einem Löffel Zucker** |
| | | with just one spoon of sugar |
| | *(means)* | **er geht mit einem Stock** |
| | | he walks with a stick |
| | | **mit ihr ist heute nichts anzufangen** |
| | | you won't get anywhere with her today |
| BY | *(means)* | **mit dem Auto/Flugzeug/Zug** |
| | | by car/plane/train |
| IN | *(time)* | **mit der Zeit** |
| | | in (the course of) time |
| AT | *(time)* | **mit 30 Jahren** |
| | | at 30 (years of age) |
| | *(speed)* | **mit 100 Stundenkilometern** |
| | | at 100 kilometres an hour |

**NACH**

| | | |
|---|---|---|
| TO | *(place)* | **der Zug nach Athen** |
| | | the train to Athens |
| | *(place)* | **wer geht nach Hause?** |
| | | who's going home? |
| | *(place)* | **nach rechts/links/oben/unten gehen** |
| | | to go right/left/upstairs/downstairs |
| AFTER | *(time)* | **nach der Prüfung/zwei Jahren** |
| | | after the exam/two years |
| PAST | *(time)* | **es ist 5 (Minuten) nach 3** |
| | | it's 5 (minutes) past 3 |
| | | **meiner/Ihrer Meinung nach** |
| | | in my/your opinion |

**VON**

| | | |
|---|---|---|
| FROM | *(place)* | **von Lübeck bis Hamburg** |
| | | from Lübeck to Hamburg |
| | | **von dieser Stelle aus kann man die Berge sehen** |
| | | from this position you can see the mountains |
| | | **wir holen dich vom (= von dem) Bahnhof ab** |
| | | we'll collect you from the station |
| FROM | *(time)* | **von 6 bis 9 Uhr abends** |
| | | from 6 to 9 in the evening |
| | | **vom 1. bis zum 15. Juli** |
| | | from the 1st to the 15th of July |
| OF | *(possession)* | **ein Freund von mir** |
| | | a friend of mine |
| | | **jeder/viele von uns** |
| | | each/many of us |

Note that in colloquial language, von is often used instead of the genitive case:

**die Erwartungen von deutschen Teenagern (= deutscher Teenager)**
the expectations of German teenagers

| BY | *(agent)* | **dieses Dorf wurde vom Feind zerstört**<br>this village was destroyed by the enemy<br>**eine Platte von den Beatles**<br>a record by the Beatles |
|---|---|---|
| **ZU** | | |
| TO | *(place)* | **bitte, komm zu mir!**<br>come to me, please!<br>**wie komme ich zur (= zu der) Post?**<br>how do I get to the post office?<br>**er muss zum (= zu dem) Arzt**<br>he has to go to the doctor's |
| AT | *(place)* | **zu Hause sein**<br>to be at home |
| | *(time)* | **zu Ostern/Weihnachten**<br>at Easter/Christmas<br>**zurzeit**<br>at present |
| | *(price)* | **zu 30 Euro das Stück**<br>at 30 euros each<br>**zum halben Preis**<br>at half price |
| FOR | *(time)* | **zum ersten Mal**<br>for the first time |
| ON | *(manner)* | **zu Fuß**<br>on foot |
| — | *(+ gerund)* | **sie kam kaum zum Schreiben**<br>she hardly got round to writing |

**B WITH THE ACCUSATIVE ONLY**

BIS

| TILL | *(time)* | **bis nächstes Jahr!** |
| | | till next year! |

Note that 'not till' is translated by erst:

**ich fahre erst morgen in Urlaub**
I'm not going on holiday till tomorrow

| | *(idiom)* | **bis bald/später!** |
| | | see you soon/later! |
| BY | *(time)* | **bis morgen** |
| | | by tomorrow |

Note that bis is often coupled with other prepositions, which then determine the case of the following noun or pronoun:

**bis zum 10. Juni**
by the 10th of June
**bis an die Grenze**
as far as the border

*but:*

**bis München**
as far as Munich

**bis auf dich sind wir alle fertig**
we're all ready except for you

DURCH

| THROUGH | *(place)* | **er rannte durch das Dorf** |
| | | he ran through the village |
| | *(agent)* | **ich habe sie durch meinen Vater kennengelernt** |
| | | I got to know her through my father |
| | *(means)* | **nur durch Fleiß macht man Fortschritte** |
| | | only through hard work do you make progress |
| BY | *(passive)* | **durch Zufall** |
| | | by chance |
| | | **die Ernte wurde durch Hagel vernichtet** |
| | | the harvest was destroyed by hail |

## PREPOSITIONS

### ENTLANG

*(usually with accusative)*

| ALONG | *(place)* | **sie rannte die Straße entlang** |
| | | she ran along the street |

### FÜR

| FOR | *(person)* | **ich habe ein Geschenk für dich!** |
| | | I have a present for you! |
| | *(time)* | **sie ging für ein Jahr ins Ausland** |
| | | she went abroad for a year |
| | *(price)* | **wir haben es für 500 Euro bekommen** |
| | | we bought it for 500 euros |

### GEGEN

| AGAINST | *(place)* | **er lehnte sich gegen die Mauer** |
| | | he leant against the wall |
| | | **was hast du gegen mich/diese Idee?** |
| | | what have you got against me/this idea? |
| ABOUT | *(time)* | **gegen 6 Uhr** |
| | | about 6 o'clock |
| TOWARDS | *(time)* | **gegen Abend/Ende des Monats** |
| | | towards evening/the end of the month |
| IN RETURN FOR | | **gegen Quittung bekommen Sie Ihr Geld zurück** |
| | | you'll get your money back in return for your receipt |
| CONTRARY TO | | **gegen alle Erwartungen** |
| | | contrary to all expectations |
| FOR | | **haben Sie Tabletten gegen Halsweh?** |
| | | do you have any tablets for a sore throat? |

### OHNE

| WITHOUT | | **sie kam ohne ihre Eltern** |
| | | she came without her parents |

**PER**

*(usually without a following article)*

| BY | | **per Post** |
| | | by post |
| – | *(idiom)* | **ich bin per du mit ihr** |
| | | I'm on first name terms with her |

**PRO**

*(usually without a following article)*

| **zwei Mal pro Tag** | **50 Euro pro Stück** |
| twice a day | 50 euros each |

**UM**

| ROUND | *(place)* | **er fährt gerade um die Ecke** |
| | | he's just driving round the corner |
| | *(place)* | **wir alle standen um sie (herum)** |
| | | we all stood round her |
| AT | *(time)* | **um 11 Uhr** |
| | | at 11 o'clock |
| AROUND | *(time)* | **diese Kirche wurde um 1400 gebaut** |
| | | this church was built around 1400 |
| BY | *(amount)* | **um fünf Euro billiger** |
| | | cheaper by five euros |

## C WITH THE DATIVE OR ACCUSATIVE

**1** A number of German prepositions are followed by either
the dative or accusative case. The most common are:

| an | on(to), against, to, at, in |
| auf | (down) on(to) |
| hinter | behind |
| in | in(to) |

| | |
|---|---|
| neben | next to, beside |
| über | above, over |
| unter | under(neath), below |
| vor | in front of, before |
| zwischen | between |

As a general rule, the dative is used where the position or location of a person, thing or action is signified. wo? is thus the question word most likely to prompt a statement of this kind.

| **wo ist Katrin?** | → | **sie sitzt auf dem Sofa** |
|---|---|---|
| where is Katrin? | | she's sitting on the sofa |

| **wo hängt der Spiegel?** | → | **er hängt an der Tür** |
|---|---|---|
| where's the mirror (hanging)? | | it's (hanging) on the door |

| **wo kann man hier einen Spaziergang machen?** | → | **im Park kann man einen Spaziergang machen** |
|---|---|---|
| where can you go for a walk here? | | you can go for a walk in the park |

The accusative indicates movement to, or in the direction of, a new position. wohin? is therefore the question word most likely to elicit a statement of this kind.

| **wohin fließt der Fluss?** | → | **er fließt in den Bodensee** |
|---|---|---|
| where does the river flow to? | | it flows into Lake Constance |

| **wohin ist die Katze gesprungen?** | → | **sie ist auf den Kühlschrank gesprungen** |
|---|---|---|
| where did the cat jump to? | | it jumped onto the fridge |

The following short forms are very common, both in spoken and written German:

| | |
|---|---|
| ans (= an das) | am (= an dem) |
| ins (= in das) | im (= in dem) |

Other examples of abbreviation:

| | |
|---|---|
| aufs (= auf das) | auf'm (= auf dem) *(used only in colloquial speech)* |
| hinters (= hinter das) | hinterm (= hinter dem) |
| übers (= über das) | überm (= über dem) |
| unters (= unter das) | unterm (= unter dem) |
| vors (= vor das) | vorm (= vor dem) |

Note that there are no standard short forms with neben and zwischen, although in colloquial German, nebens (= neben das) is possible.

*For the combination of prepositions with pronouns (darin, darauf, etc) see p 91.*

**2** The following examples begin in each case with a pair of sentences to make clear the essential difference between these prepositions in their accusative and dative use:

AN

| **ACCUSATIVE** | **DATIVE** |
|---|---|
| sie klebte das Foto an die Tür | das Foto klebt an der Tür |
| she stuck the photo on the door | the photo is stuck on the door |
| wir fliegen jeden Sommer ans Mittelmeer | normalerweise zelten wir am Mittelmeer |
| every summer we fly to the Mediterranean | we normally camp on the Mediterranean |

| | | |
|---|---|---|
| ON *(time)* | | am Sonntag |
| | | on Sunday |
| | | am 31. August |
| | | on the 31st of August |
| IN *(time)* | | am Morgen/Abend |
| | | in the morning/evening |
| *(idiom)* | | an Ihrer Stelle |
| | | in your position |
| AT *(time)* | | am Wochenende |
| | | at the weekend |
| *(place)* | | an einer Schule/Universität |
| | | at a school/university |

## PREPOSITIONS

### AUF

**ACCUSATIVE**

**stellen Sie bitte Ihr Gepäck nicht auf das Bett!**
please don't put your luggage on the bed

**sie ist gerade auf ihr Zimmer gegangen**
she's just gone to her room

| | | |
|---|---|---|
| TO *(place)* | **auf den Markt gehen** | to go to the market |
| | **er zieht aufs Land** | he's moving to the country(side) |

| | | |
|---|---|---|
| IN *(manner)* | **auf diese Weise** | in this way |
| *(language)* | **auf Deutsch** | in German |
| FOR *(time)* | **auf einige Tage** | for a few days |

**auf jeden Fall**
whatever happens
**auf einen Baum klettern**
to climb a tree

**DATIVE**

**mein Koffer steht aber nicht auf dem Bett**
but my suitcase isn't on the bed

**auf ihrem Zimmer schläft sie sicher bald ein**
she'll soon fall asleep in her room

| | | |
|---|---|---|
| AT *(place)* | **auf dem Markt sein** | to be at the market |
| IN *(place)* | **er wohnt auf dem Lande** | he lives in the country(side) |
| | **auf einem Bild/der Welt** | in a picture/the world |

| | | |
|---|---|---|
| FROM *(place)* | **auf 3 Kilometer zu sehen/hören** | visible/audible from 3 kilometres |

## HINTER

| ACCUSATIVE | DATIVE |
|---|---|
| **geh nicht hinter das Haus!** | **ein Teich liegt hinter dem Haus** |
| don't go behind the house! | there's a pond behind the house |
| **bitte setzen Sie sich hinter mich!** | **nun sitzen alle hinter mir** |
| please sit behind me | now everyone's sitting behind me |

|  |  |  |
|---|---|---|
| AFTER *(place)* | **die erste Station hinter Stuttgart** | the first stop after Stuttgart |
| *(chasing)* | **die Behörden sind hinter ihnen her** | the authorities are after them |
| BEYOND *(place)* | **einige Kilometer hinter der Grenze** | a few kilometres beyond the border |

## IN

| ACCUSATIVE | DATIVE |
|---|---|
| **unsere Katze kommt gern in die Küche** | **unsere Katze schläft gern in der Küche** |
| our cat likes coming into the kitchen | our cat likes sleeping in the kitchen |
| **er geht in die Kirche/ins Kino/in den Zoo** | **er ist in der Kirche/im Kino/im Zoo** |
| he's going to church/to the cinema/the zoo | he's in church/at the cinema/the zoo |

## PREPOSITIONS

| TO *(place)* | in die Alpen/die USA/ ins Ausland reisen<br>to travel to the Alps/ the USA/abroad | IN *(place)* | in den Alpen/den USA/ im Ausland arbeiten<br>to work in the Alps/the USA/abroad |

Note the following points:

With most countries the relevant prepositions are nach and in:

| | nach Schweden reisen<br>to travel to Sweden | | in Schweden arbeiten<br>to work in Sweden |

Compare 'I've never been to France/Switzerland' and ich war noch nie in Frankreich/in der Schweiz

| | in Urlaub fahren/ gehen<br>to go on holiday | | im Urlaub sein<br>to be on holiday |
| IN *(place)* | gehen Sie in diese Richtung!<br>go in this direction | | gehen Sie in dieser Richtung weiter!<br>keep going in this direction |

Note the following:

**wir fahren jetzt Richtung Moskau**
we're travelling now in the direction of Moscow

**schreib ihre Adresse in dein Notizbuch!**
write her address (down) in your notebook

| IN *(clothes)* | in einen blauen Anzug gekleidet<br>dressed in a blue suit | | in Stiefeln/Blau gehen<br>to wear boots/blue |
| INTO *(time)* | es dauert bis spät in die Nacht (hinein)<br>it goes on (well) into the night | | |
| | | IN *(time)* | in einer Minute<br>in one minute |

|  |  |
|---|---|
|  | **in der Nacht**<br>in the night |
|  | **im November/Herbst**<br>in November/autumn |
|  | **im Jahre 1967**<br>in 1967 |
| IN<br>*(+ gerund)* | **im Vorbeigehen**<br>**lächelte sie mich an**<br>she smiled at me in passing |
| AT *(activity)* | **gut in Physik**<br>good at physics |
| ON *(idioms)* | **im Durchschnitt**<br>on average |
|  | **im Gegenteil**<br>on the contrary |
|  | **im Ganzen**<br>on the whole |

## NEBEN

| ACCUSATIVE | DATIVE |
|---|---|
| **sie setzte sich neben mich**<br>she sat down beside me | **sie saß neben mir**<br>she was sitting beside me |
|  | **er ging neben mir her**<br>he walked beside me |
|  | *compare with:* |
|  | **neben meinen Schuhen sind deine**<br>   **sehr billig**<br>compared with my shoes yours are very cheap |
|  | IN ADDI-  **neben diesen Kosten**<br>  TION TO    **muss ich noch**<br>      **Mehrwertsteuer**<br>      **zahlen**<br>in addition to these costs I also have to pay VAT |

ÜBER

**ACCUSATIVE**

**fahren Sie links über den Kanal**
go left over the canal
**ein Panzerwagen fährt über das Feld**
a tank is driving across the field

| | |
|---|---|
| VIA *(place)* | **wir fliegen über die Türkei nach Moskau** <br> we're flying to Moscow via Turkey |
| THROUGH *(agent)* | **das habe ich über einen Freund bekommen** <br> I got it through a friend |
| OVER *(time)* | **über eine Stunde** <br> over (= more than) an hour |
| | **übers Wochenende** <br> over the weekend |
| | **das ganze Jahr über** <br> all year round |
| ON/ ABOUT | **ein Buch über die deutsche Grammatik** <br> a book on German grammar |
| FOR | **ein Scheck über 100 Euro** <br> a cheque for 100 euros |

**DATIVE**

**über dem Kanal lag dichter Nebel**
there was a thick fog over the canal
**ein Hubschrauber kreiste über dem Haus**
a helicopter was circling over the house

| | |
|---|---|
| OVER *(seniority)* | **sie steht über uns allen** <br> she is over us all |
| *but:* | **seit über einem Jahr wohne ich hier** <br> I've lived here for over a year |
| ABOVE | **über dem Durchschnitt** <br> above average |

## UNTER

**ACCUSATIVE**

**Das Flugzeug flog unter die Brücke**
the plane flew under(neath) the
  bridge

**Er legte sich unter den Baum**
he lay down underneath the tree

**DATIVE**

**ich warte schon eine Stunde unter
  dieser Brücke**
I've been waiting for an hour under
  this bridge

**die Kinder spielten unter dem Baum**
the children were playing under the
  tree

| | |
|---|---|
| UNDER *(seniority)* | **Sie haben 2 Arbeiter unter sich** you have 2 workers under you |
| UNDER *(time)* | **Kinder unter 10 Jahren** children under 10 (years of age) |
| IN *(idiom)* | **unter Umständen** in certain circumstances |
| UNDER *(less than)* | **unter einem Kilo/Euro** under a kilo/one euro |
| BELOW | **unter dem Meeresspiegel** below sea level **unter dem Durchschnitt** below average |
| AMONG | **unter ihren Freunden** among her friends **unter anderem** among other things |
| ON *(idiom)* | **unter der Bedingung, dass …** on condition that … |

BY          **was versteht man unter Onlinewerbung?**
            what do you understand by 'online advertising'?

## VOR

| ACCUSATIVE | DATIVE |
|---|---|
| **er setzt sich sofort vor den Fernseher** | **er sitzt den ganzen Abend vor dem Fernseher** |
| he immediately sits (down) in front of the television | he sits all evening in front of the television |

**vor ihm lag nichts als Schlamm**
ahead of him lay nothing but mud

| BEFORE *(order)* | **A kommt vor B** |
| | A comes before B |
| BEFORE *(time)* | **vor dem Krieg** |
| | before the war |
| | **vor dem 19. November** |
| | before the 19th of November |
| AGO *(time)* | **vor einem Jahr/einiger Zeit** |
| | a year/some time ago |
| TO *(time)* | **20 (Minuten) vor 6** |
| | 20 (minutes) to 6 |
| OF *(cause)* | **vor Hunger/Langeweile sterben** |
| | to die of hunger/boredom |
| WITH *(cause)* | **vor Kälte zittern** |
| | to shiver with cold |
| | **grün vor Neid** |
| | green with envy |
| ABOVE *(idiom)* | **vor allem/allen Dingen** |
| | above all |

TO     **er murmelte vor sich hin**
*(idiom)*   he was mumbling to
          himself

ZWISCHEN

| **ACCUSATIVE** | **DATIVE** |
|---|---|
| **der Turm fiel zwischen zwei große Lastwagen** | **der Turm zwischen den jungen Bäumen steht noch** |
| the tower fell between two big lorries | the tower between the young trees is still standing |

                        BETWEEN   **zwischen 4 und 5 Uhr**
                        *(time)*     between 4 and 5 o'clock
                                      **Kinder zwischen 5 und 10 Jahren**
                                        children between 5 and 10 (years of age)

Note the following:

    **er ist zwischen 50 und 60 Jahre alt**
    he's between 50 and 60 (years old)

                            *(quantity)*   **zwischen 10 und 12 Euro pro Stunde**
                                        between 10 and 12 euros an hour
                                        **was ist der Unterschied zwischen Butter und Margarine?**
                                        what's the difference between butter and margarine?

 **WITH THE GENITIVE**

ANHAND
BY MEANS OF               **er erläuterte seine Theorie anhand eines Beispiels**
                        he explained his theory by means of an example

## PREPOSITIONS

### AUSSERHALB

| | | |
|---|---|---|
| OUTSIDE | *(place)* | **eine Kirche steht außerhalb des Dorf(e)s**<br>there's a church outside the village |
| | *(time)* | **außerhalb der Arbeitszeit**<br>outside working hours |

### DIESSEITS

| | | |
|---|---|---|
| ON THIS<br>SIDE OF | *(place)* | **diesseits der Straße**<br>on this side of the street |

### INNERHALB

| | | |
|---|---|---|
| INSIDE | *(place)* | **innerhalb der Raumkapsel**<br>inside the space capsule |
| WITHIN | *(time)* | **innerhalb einer Sekunde**<br>within a second |

### JENSEITS

| | | |
|---|---|---|
| ON THE<br>OTHER SIDE<br>OF | *(place)* | **jenseits des Flusses**<br>on the other side of the river |

### KRAFT

| | |
|---|---|
| BY VIRTUE OF | **kraft seines Amtes**<br>by virtue of his office |

### MITTELS

| | |
|---|---|
| BY MEANS OF | **mittels eines Zweitschlüssels**<br>by means of a duplicate key |

### STATT

| | |
|---|---|
| INSTEAD OF | **statt des Bürgermeisters**<br>instead of the mayor |

| | |
|---|---|
| *(idiom)* | **stattdessen**<br>instead of this/that |

**UM...WILLEN**

FOR... SAKE

**um ihrer Mutter willen**
for her mother's sake
**um Gottes/Himmels willen!**
for God's/Heaven's sake!

**WÄHREND**

DURING

**während unseres Aufenthaltes in Italien**
during our stay in Italy
**während dieser Zeit**
during this period

##  E WITH THE GENITIVE OR DATIVE

**DANK**

THANKS TO

**dank meines guten Gedächtnisses** *(gen)*
*or*
**dank meinem guten Gedächtnis** *(dat)*
thanks to my good memory

**TROTZ**

IN SPITE OF

**trotz strömenden Regens** *(gen)*
*or*
**trotz strömendem Regen** *(dat)*
in spite of the pouring rain

The use of the dative with trotz is generally regarded as colloquial.
Note, however the following expressions, which are standard German:

| | |
|---|---|
| **trotzdem** | **trotz allem/alledem** |
| nonetheless | in spite of everything |

## PREPOSITIONS

WEGEN

BECAUSE OF   **wegen der hohen Preise** *(gen)*

*or*

**wegen den hohen Preisen** *(dat)*
because of the high prices
**wegen meines Kindes** *(gen)*

*or*

**wegen meinem Kind** *(dat)*
for my child's sake

Note that the use of the dative with wegen is generally regarded as colloquial.

Note the following forms with personal pronouns:

**meinetwegen**      **seinetwegen** *etc*
for my sake        for his *etc* sake

Used colloquially, meinetwegen means 'as far as I'm concerned':

**meinetwegen kann er auch mitkommen**
as far as I'm concerned, he can come along too

# 9 CONJUNCTIONS

Conjunctions link words, phrases or clauses:

**vor und hinter dem Haus**
in front of *and* behind the house

**schön aber gefährlich**
beautiful *but* dangerous

**nimm meinen Schirm, damit du nicht nass wirst**
take my umbrella *so that* you don't get wet

They fall into two categories, coordinating and subordinating.

## A COORDINATING CONJUNCTIONS

### 1 Definition

These link two similar words or groups of words (eg nouns, pronouns, adjectives, adverbs, prepositions, phrases or clauses).

### 2 The principal coordinating conjunctions:

| | | |
|---|---|---|
| aber | denn | oder |
| but | because | or |
| und | sondern | sowie |
| and | but | as well as |

*For the use of commas with conjunctions, see pp 249–50.*

### 3 Word order

When introducing clauses they are followed by the normal word order:

**ich esse gern Käse, aber ich trinke nicht gern Milch**
I like cheese but I don't like milk

**gehen wir ins Konzert oder bleiben wir zu Hause?**
shall we go to the concert, or shall we stay at home?

**sie schlief nicht ein, sondern (sie) lag hellwach im Bett**
she didn't go to sleep, but lay wide awake in bed

Note that sondern is only used of two incompatible ideas:

**nicht schwarz, sondern weiß**          **nicht klug, sonder dumm**
not black but white                       not clever but stupid

## 4 Conjunctions consisting of two parts:

| | |
|---|---|
| sowohl ... als auch | nicht nur ... sondern auch |
| both ... and | not only ... but also |
| entweder ... oder | weder ... noch |
| either ... or | neither ... nor |

**sowohl deine Mutter als auch ich sind dagegen**
both your mother and I are against it

**nicht nur das Essen, sondern auch das Bier war sehr teuer**
not only the food but also the beer was very expensive

**entweder er oder sie muss weg**
either he or she will have to go

**weder Rom noch Neapel hat ihnen gefallen**
they liked neither Rome nor Naples

## 5 Adverbs

Some adverbs also function as coordinating conjunctions. In such cases the order of the following subject and finite verb is reversed. Among the most common of these adverbs are:

| | | |
|---|---|---|
| also | außerdem | deshalb |
| so, therefore | in any case | therefore |
| inzwischen | sonst | trotzdem |
| meanwhile | otherwise | despite that |

**ich stehe morgen früh auf, ich muss also jetzt gehen**
**ich stehe morgen früh auf, also muss ich jetzt gehen**
I'm getting up early tomorrow, so I'll have to go now

**er steht heute unter Stress; er wäre sonst gekommen**
**er steht heute unter Stress; sonst wäre er gekommen**
he's under pressure today, otherwise he would have come

**sie ist 35; sie benimmt sich trotzdem wie ein Kind**
**sie ist 35; trotzdem benimmt sie sich wie ein Kind**
she's 35; despite that she behaves like a child

## B SUBORDINATING CONJUNCTIONS

### 1 Definition

These join a subordinate clause to another clause, in particular a main clause. The finite verb comes at the end of a subordinate clause. (The only exception is noted in section 3b.)

### 2 The principal subordinating conjunctions:

| | | |
|---|---|---|
| dass | als | bevor/ehe |
| that | when | before |
| nachdem | seit(dem) | während |
| after | since | while |
| wenn | als ob | damit |
| if, when(ever) | as if | so that |
| da/weil | sodass | sobald |
| because | with the result that | as soon as |
| obwohl/obgleich | ohne (...) zu | um (...) zu |
| although | without | in order to |

**bitte sag ihm, dass ich große Lust dazu hätte**
please tell him that I'd love to do it

**die Firma ging pleite, als sie 50 war**
the firm went bust when she was 50

*or:*

**als sie 50 war, ging die Firma pleite**
when she was 50 the firm went bust

**wenn wir nur Zeit hätten, würden wir so viel tun**
if only we had the time we'd do so much

**wenn ich dir begegne, siehst du immer so traurig aus**
when(ever) I see you, you always look so sad

**sie ging, als ob sie blind wäre**
she was walking as if she were blind

Note that sie ging, als wäre sie blind is also possible.

**mein Schirm war kaputt, sodass ich bis auf die Haut nass wurde**
my umbrella was broken, so I got soaked

Note the difference between sodass and damit:

**steh auf, damit ich dich sehe**
stand up so (that) I can see you

Note that ohne (...) zu and um (...) zu + infinitive can only be used
when the (implicit) subject is the same in each clause:

**ohne ein Wort zu sagen, schlich er aus dem Haus**
without saying a word, he crept out of the house

**ich koche selber, um Geld zu sparen**
I cook for myself to save money

## 3 Omission

On occasion, dass or wenn may be omitted.

a) When the subordinate clause in question comes after the main
clause, the finite verb in it occupies its 'normal' position:

**bitte sag ihm, ich hätte große Lust dazu**
please tell him I'd love to do it

**b)** When the subordinate clause comes before the main clause, the finite verb in it is the first word of the sentence:

**hätten wir nur Zeit, würden wir so viel tun**
had we only the time, we'd do so much

Note that in all these examples the two clauses are still separated by a comma.

# 4 Interrogatives

Interrogatives (eg **was?**, **welcher?** and **wie?**) and **ob** function as subordinating conjunctions in indirect questions:

**der Polizist fragte mich, ob ich etwas gehört hätte**
the policeman asked me if I had heard anything

**dann fragte er mich, was ich gehört hätte**
then he asked me what I had heard

*See also* pp 244–45.

# 10 NUMBERS AND QUANTITY

## A CARDINAL NUMBERS

| | | | |
|---|---|---|---|
| 0 | null | 30 | dreißig |
| 1 | eins | 40 | vierzig |
| 2 | zwei | 50 | fünfzig |
| 3 | drei | 60 | sechzig |
| 4 | vier | 70 | siebzig |
| 5 | fünf | 80 | achtzig |
| 6 | sechs | 90 | neunzig |
| 7 | sieben | 100 | hundert |
| 8 | acht | 101 | hunderteins |
| 9 | neun | 130 | hundertdreißig |
| 10 | zehn | 200 | zweihundert |
| 11 | elf | 257 | zweihundertsiebenundfünfzig |
| 12 | zwölf | | |
| 13 | dreizehn | 1 000 | tausend |
| 14 | vierzehn | 1 001 | tausend(und)eins |
| 15 | fünfzehn | 1 234 | tausendzweihundertvier
unddreißig |
| 16 | sechzehn | | |
| 17 | siebzehn | 1 990 | neunzehnhundertneunzig
*(date)* |
| 18 | achtzehn | | |
| 19 | neunzehn | 2 000 | zweitausend |
| 20 | zwanzig | 10 000 | zehntausend |
| 21 | einundzwanzig | 1 000 000 | eine Million |
| 26 | sechsundzwanzig | 1 198 269 | eine Million hundertachtund
neunzigtausendzweihundert
neunundsechzig |
| | | 2 000 000 | zwei Millionen |
| | | 1 000 000 000 | eine Milliarde |
| | | 1 000 000 000 000 | eine Billion |

**a)** The cardinal number 1 has the form eins:

- in arithmetic:

  **eins plus eins gleich zwei**
  one plus one equals two

- in compound numbers, when it is the last item:

  | **zweihunderteins** | *but:* | **zweihunderteinundfünfzig** |
  |---|---|---|
  | two hundred and one | | two hundred and fifty one |

- after a noun:

  | **Zimmer eins** | **Seite eins** |
  |---|---|
  | room one | page one |

**b)** When used before a noun it is declined like the indefinite article (*see* **p 23**), but distinguished from it by being stressed in speech:

**ich habe bloß einen Euro gespart!**
I only saved *one* euro!

However, if preceded by the definite article it is declined like a normal adjective (*see* **p 62**):

**den einen Schein hat er schon, den anderen aber nicht**
he's got one certificate already, but not the other

---

## Note

Note the following expressions:

- time expressions:

  | **um ein Uhr** | *but:* | **es ist eins** |
  |---|---|---|
  | at one o'clock | | it is one o'clock |

- expressions combined with zwei:

  **jeden Tag liest er ein oder zwei Zeitungen**
  every day he reads one or two papers

c) When used as a pronoun, 1 is declined like dieser:

**einer der Filme**          **eines/eins der Bücher**
one of the films             one of the books

d) zwei is sometimes replaced by zwo when it might be mistaken for drei (eg on the telephone).

e) 'in twos', 'in threes' *etc* (up to 12) is translated by zu zweit, zu dritt, zu viert, zu fünft *etc*.

f) 'tens', 'twenties' *etc* as denominations of stamps, coins and notes add the ending -er but are otherwise indeclinable, except for the dative plural:

**eine Zwanziger (Marke)**    **ein Zwanziger (Schein)**
a 20-cent stamp              a 20-euro note

g) 'dozens/hundreds/thousands of' is translated by Dutzende/ Hunderte/Tausende von

h) Where English uses a comma in writing thousands *etc* German uses either a full stop or a space:
1.500.000
1 500 000
1,500,000

The German for a million, a thousand million and a billion takes the plural form:

**zwei Millionen Euro/Wörter**
two million euros/words

**B ORDINAL NUMBERS**

Note that the following numbers are usually preceded by an article *etc* and are always declined.

| | |
|---|---|
| 1st | erst- |
| 2nd | zweit- |
| 3rd | dritt- |
| 4th | viert- |
| 5th | fünft- |
| 6th | sechst- |
| 7th | siebt- |
| 8th | acht- |
| 9th | neunt- |
| 10th | zehnt- |
| 11th | elft- |
| 12th | zwölft- |
| 13th | dreizehnt- |
| 14th | vierzehnt- |
| 15th | fünfzehnt- |
| 16th | sechzehnt- |
| 17th | siebzehnt- |
| 18th | achtzehnt- |
| 19th | neunzehnt- |
| 20th | zwanzigst- |
| 21st | einundzwanzigst- |
| 30th | dreißigst- |
| 100th | hundertst- |
| 101st | hunderterst- |
| 200th | zweihundertst- |
| 1000th | tausendst- |
| 10,000th | zehntausendst- |
| 1,000,000th | millionst- |

a) ordinal numbers agree with the noun following them in gender and case:

**meine zwölfte Stelle**
my twelfth job

**kennen Sie ihren dritten Mann?**
do you know her third husband?

b) when written in figures, ordinals are followed by a full stop:

**Beethovens 9. Sinfonie**
Beethoven's 9th symphony

**heute ist der 23. Oktober**
today is the 23rd of October

After the names of kings *etc* Roman numerals with punctuation, or, less commonly, the full form in words, are used:

**das gehörte Karl V./Karl dem Fünften**
that belonged to Charles V/Charles the Fifth

##  C FRACTIONS AND PROPORTIONS

### 1 Fractions

Fractions are formed by substituting the -te ending of ordinal numerals with -tel. They are neuter nouns, but are only inflected in the genitive singular, adding -s:

**ein Drittel**
a third ($^1/_3$)

**vier Fünftel**
four fifths (4/5)

**zweieinhalb**
two and a half (2½)

but note that 'half' is translated by die Hälfte (noun) or halb- (adjective or adverb):

**die Hälfte der Studenten**
half the students

**die größere Hälfte**
the larger half

**eine halbe Stunde**
half an hour

**ein halbes Kilo Äpfel**
half a kilo of apples

**halb so viel**
half as much

**halb tot**
half dead

Note the expression:

**anderthalb/eineinhalb**
one and a half

## 2 Decimals

The English decimal point is expressed as a comma in German:

**zwei Komma fünf (2,5)**
two point five (2.5)

## 3 Arithmetic

| | | |
|---|---|---|
| *Addition:* | **zwei** plus/und **drei gleich fünf** | 2 + 3 = 5 |
| *Subtraction:* | **sieben** minus/weniger **eins gleich sechs** | 7 − 1 = 6 |
| *Multiplication:* | **vier** mal **zwei gleich acht** | 4 × 2 = 8 |
| *Division:* | **neun** (geteilt) durch **drei gleich drei** | 9 ÷ 3 = 3 |
| *Square:* | **zwei** hoch **zwei gleich vier** | $2^2 = 4$ |

Note that ist, sind or macht are alternatives to gleich.

 **D MEASUREMENTS AND PRICES**

## 1 Measurements

a) *Dimensions*

**dieses Zimmer ist 4 Meter (4 m) lang und 3 Meter 70 (3,70 m) breit**
this room is 4 metres long and 3.70 metres wide

**das Loch ist 30 cm tief**
the hole is 30 cm deep

**er ist 1,80m groß**
he's 1.80 metres tall

b) *Distance*

**wie weit ist es von hier bis Kassel?**
how far is it from here to Kassel?

**bis Kassel sind es bloß 3 Kilometer**
it's only 3 kilometres to Kassel

**Kassel liegt 3 km von hier (entfernt)**
Kassel is 3 km (away) from here

## 2 Prices

**was kosten die Umschläge?**
how much are the envelopes?

**sie kosten zwei Euro zehn (€2,10)**
they're 2 euros 10

**diese Bananen haben mich 3 Euro gekostet!**
these bananas cost me 3 euros!

**75 Cent das/pro Stück**
75 cents each

**5 Euro das/pro Kilo**
5 euros a kilo

**Weinbrand zu 10 Euro die/pro Flasche**
brandy at 10 euros a bottle

**das macht 34 Euro neunzig (€34,90)**
that makes/comes to 34 euros 90

# 11 EXPRESSIONS OF TIME

## A THE TIME

**wie spät ist es?**
what's the time?

**wie viel Uhr ist es?**
what's the time?

**wie viel Uhr haben Sie?**
what time do you make it?

a) *full hours*

**es ist ein Uhr/eins**
it's 1 o'clock

**es ist Mittag/Mitternacht**
it's 12 noon/midnight

b) *half-hours* (note the difference from English)

**es ist halb vier**
it's half past three

**es ist vier Uhr dreißig**
it's half past four

**es ist halb eins (nachts/nachmittags)**
it's 12.30 (at night/in the afternoon)

c) *quarter-hours*

**es ist Viertel nach elf/viertel zwölf** *(S. Germany)*
it's 11.15

**es ist Viertel vor zehn/drei viertel zehn** *(S. Germany)*
it's 9.45

d) *minutes*

**es ist acht Minuten nach neun**
it's 9.08

**es ist sechzehn Minuten vor sechs**
it's 5.44

**es ist fünf vor/nach halb drei**
it's 2.25/2.35

**es ist zwanzig vor sieben**
it's 6.40

Note that Uhr is sometimes omitted, as is Minuten

e) *a.m. and p.m.*

**es ist zehn Uhr vormittags**
it's 10 a.m.

**es ist drei Uhr nachmittags**
it's 3 p.m.

Note:

**es ist zwei Uhr nachts**
it's 2 a.m.

**es ist acht Uhr abends**
it's 8 p.m.

f) The 24 hour clock is especially used in official announcements, TV and radio announcements, timetables *etc* but can also be used in ordinary speech:

**unser Zug fährt um 20 Uhr**
our train leaves at 8 p.m.

**die Vorstellung fängt um 19.30 Uhr** (spoken: neunzehn Uhr dreißig) **an**
the performance starts at 7.30 p.m.

## B THE DATE

### 1 Names of months, days and seasons

a) *Months* (die Monate)

| | |
|---|---|
| Januar | January |
| Februar | February |
| März | March |
| April | April |
| Mai | May |
| Juni | June |
| Juli | July |
| August | August |
| September | September |
| Oktober | October |
| November | November |
| Dezember | December |

b) *Days of the week* (die Wochentage)

| | |
|---|---|
| Montag | Monday |
| Dienstag | Tuesday |
| Mittwoch | Wednesday |
| Donnerstag | Thursday |
| Freitag | Friday |
| Samstag | Saturday |
| Sonnabend *(N. Germany)* | Saturday |
| Sonntag | Sunday |

c) *Seasons* (die Jahreszeiten)

| | |
|---|---|
| der Frühling | spring |
| der Sommer | summer |
| der Herbst | autumn |
| der Winter | winter |

| **im Juni** | **am Mittwoch** | **im Herbst** |
|---|---|---|
| in June | on Wednesday | in the autumn |

## 2 Dates

a) Ordinal numbers are used for the dates of the month, as in English, but 'of' is not translated:

**der 1. (*spoken:* erste) Mai**          **am 11. (*spoken:* elften) April**
the first of May                          on the 11th of April

Note that dates on letters and cards are usually written:

**Dortmund, (den) 3.7.2008** (*read* **den dritten Siebten zweitausendacht**)

*or*

**Dortmund, den 3. Juli 2008**

b) 'what's the date today?' is translated as:

**der Wievielte ist heute?** *or*
**den Wievielten haben wir heute?**

## EXPRESSIONS OF TIME

c) With years, German either uses no preposition or the phrase im Jahr(e) + date:

**wir haben uns 1964/im Jahr(e) 1964 kennengelernt**
we got to know each other in 1964

d) Year dates are read as multiples of a hundred, except for years beginning with 10- and 20-:

|       | 1100 | **elfhundert** |
|-------|------|----------------|
|       | 1984 | **neunzehnhundertvierundachtzig** |
| *but:* | 1066 | **tausendsechsundsechzig** |
|       | 2001 | **zweitausend(und)eins** |

e) On wine labels years take an invariable -er ending:

**1976er Piesporter Michelsberg**

## C IDIOMATIC EXPRESSIONS

| | |
|---|---|
| **um 6 Uhr** | at 6 o'clock |
| **um 6 Uhr herum** *(colloquial)* | round about 6 o'clock |
| **gegen 10 Uhr** | about/getting on for 10 o'clock |
| **um Mitternacht** | at midnight |
| **gegen Mittag** | towards/around midday |
| **Punkt 3 Uhr** | on the stroke of three |
| **es ist genau 3 Uhr** | it's exactly 3 o'clock |
| **es ist 5 Uhr vorbei** | it's past 5 o'clock |
| **ab 7 Uhr** | from 7 o'clock on(wards) |
| **von 9 bis 5 Uhr** | from 9 to 5 o'clock |
| **bleib bis 2 Uhr!** | stay till 2 o'clock! |
| **das muss bis 2 Uhr fertig sein** | that must be ready by 2 o'clock! |
| **kurz vor 8 Uhr** | shortly before 8 o'clock |
| **kurz nach 9 Uhr** | shortly after 9 o'clock |

| | |
|---|---|
| eine Viertelstunde | a quarter of an hour |
| eine halbe Stunde | half an hour |
| eine Dreiviertelstunde | three quarters of an hour |
| morgens | in the morning, every morning |
| am Morgen | in the morning, every morning |
| am nächsten Morgen | (the) next morning |
| eines Morgens | one morning |
| (am) Montagmorgen | on Monday morning |
| montags morgens | on Monday mornings |
| guten Morgen! | good morning! |
| abends | in the evening, every evening |
| am Abend | in the evening, every evening |
| (am) Samstagabend | on Saturday evening |
| samstags abends | on Saturday evenings |
| eines Abends | one evening |
| jeden Abend | every evening |
| guten Abend! | good evening! |
| nachts | at night |
| über Nacht | overnight |
| Nacht für Nacht | night after night |
| eines Nachts | one night |
| gute Nacht! | good night! |
| heute | today |
| heute früh/Morgen | this morning |
| heute Nacht | last night/tonight |
| heutzutage | nowadays |
| gestern | yesterday |
| gestern Abend | yesterday evening |
| vorgestern | the day before yesterday |
| gestern vor 8 Tagen | a week ago yesterday |
| morgen | tomorrow |
| morgen früh | tomorrow morning |
| übermorgen | the day after tomorrow |
| morgen in 8 Tagen | a week tomorrow |
| von heute auf morgen | at very short notice |

| | |
|---|---|
| am Sonntag | on Sunday |
| erst am Sonntag | not till Sunday |
| sonntags, jeden Sonntag | on Sundays, every Sunday |
| täglich | every day, daily |
| alltäglich | everyday, mundane |
| in drei Tagen | in three days' time |
| tagsüber | during the day |
| letzte/nächste Woche | last/next week |
| vorletzte Woche | the week before last |
| übernächste Woche | the week after next |
| wöchentlich (Wochen-) | every week, weekly |
| während/unter der Woche | during the week |
| am/übers Wochenende | at/over the weekend |
| letzten/nächsten Monat | last/next month |
| monatlich (Monats-) | every month, monthly |
| zwei Monate lang | for two months |
| vor zwei Monaten | two months ago |
| er verdient 5 000 Euro im Monat | he earns 5,000 euros a month |
| Anfang/Ende März | at the beginning/end of March |
| letztes/nächstes Jahr | last/next year |
| jährlich (Jahres-) | every year, yearly |
| 1900/im Jahr(e) 1900 | in 1900 |
| in den 60er-Jahren | in the 60s |
| das Schaltjahr | leap year |
| im 19. Jahrhundert | in the 19th century |
| aus dem 15. Jh. | from the 15th century |
| mittelalterlich | medieval |
| 500 v.Chr. (= vor Christus) | 500 BC |
| 500 n.Chr. (= nach Christus) | 500 AD |
| Ostern | Easter |
| Pfingsten | Whitsun |
| Weihnachten | Christmas |
| Silvester | New Year's Eve |

| | |
|---|---|
| er ist 18 Jahre alt | he's 18 (years old) |
| sie ist in den Zwanzigern | she's in her twenties |
| wir sind Mitte 40 | we are in our mid 40s |
| in mittlerem Alter | middle-aged |
| in diesem Alter | at this/that age |
| das erste Mal | the first time |
| zum ersten Mal | for the first time |
| meine Uhr geht vor/nach | my watch is fast/slow |
| der Zug hat 5 Minuten Verspätung | the train is 5 minutes late |
| im Augenblick | at the moment |
| früher oder später | sooner or later |
| mit der Zeit | in (the course of) time |
| im Laufe der Zeit | in (the course of) time |
| seit einiger Zeit | for some time past |
| eine Zeit lang | for a while |
| für/auf immer | for ever |
| Zeit verbringen | to spend time |
| Zeit vergeuden | to waste time |
| sich *(dat)* Zeit für etwas *(acc)* nehmen | to make time for something |

# 12 THE SENTENCE

## A WORD ORDER

### 1 Basic word order

a) In a simple sentence the basic word order is:

*subject    finite verb  (+object/objects)   (+ complement)*

**wir essen**  
we're eating

**wir essen unser Frühstück**  
we're eating our breakfast

**wir essen unser Frühstück heute in der Küche**  
we're eating our breakfast today in the kitchen

b) If there is both a direct and an indirect object the normal order depends on whether they are nouns or pronouns

  i) two nouns (indirect, direct)

  **er gab seiner Mutter das Buch**  
  he gave his mother the book/he gave the book to his mother

  ii) pronoun (indirect), noun (direct)

  **er gab ihr das Buch**  
  he gave her the book

  iii) pronoun (direct), noun (indirect)

  **er gab es seiner Mutter**  
  he gave it to his mother

  iv) two pronouns (direct, indirect)

  **er gab es ihr**  
  he gave it to her

c) Past participles, dependent infinitives, separable prefixes and adverbial complements usually come at the end of a sentence:

**sie hat ihn in Paris zum ersten Mal gesehen**  
she saw him for the first time in Paris

**Andrea will am Samstag eine Party veranstalten**
Andrea wants to organize a party on Saturday

**du lenkst mich von meiner Arbeit ab**
you're distracting me from my work

**das Spiel geriet heute völlig außer Kontrolle**
the game got completely out of control today

Note that adverbial complements, in combination, come immediately before past participles, dependent infinitives and separable prefixes:

**das Spiel ist heute völlig außer Kontrolle geraten**
the game got completely out of control today

d) Inversion

It is far more common in German than in English to begin a sentence with something other than the subject. Not only adverbs and adverbial phrases but also direct and indirect objects regularly function in this way. Note, though, that only one such item may occur at the beginning of a given sentence.

i) If an adverb *etc* starts a sentence the finite verb must come immediately afterwards in second place (though it need not be the second word):

**leider fällt der Unterricht heute aus**
unfortunately there are no lessons today

**die Hälfte des Personals hat man schon entlassen**
they've already dismissed half the staff

**auf den müssen Sie gut aufpassen!**
you must keep a good eye on him!

ii) After inversion a pronoun subject must come directly after the finite verb:

**endlich gab er mir meine Notizen zurück**
he finally gave me back my notes

But a noun subject may either precede or follow a pronoun object:

**morgen trifft meine Frau ihn am Flughafen**
**morgen trifft ihn meine Frau am Flughafen**
my wife's meeting him at the airport tomorrow

iii) If a main clause comes second in a sentence inversion occurs:

**wenn es schneit, machen wir einen Schneemann**
if it snows we'll make a snowman

**"alles Gute!" sagte sie zynisch**
"all the best!" she said cynically

Note that after a wenn clause, dann may be added before the inverted main verb.

## 2 Subordinate Clauses

After relative pronouns (der, dessen, an dem, worauf *etc*) and subordinating conjunctions (dass, warum, obwohl *etc*) the finite verb goes to the end of the clause:

**das ist das Kind, dessen Eltern beide Teenager sind**
that's the child whose parents are both teenagers

**kennen Sie Otto, mit dem ich jahrelang in Urlaub gefahren bin?**
do you know Otto, who I've been going on holiday with for years?

When two subordinate clauses follow the same conjunction, remember to put the verb at the end of *both*:

**wenn er morgen kommt und die Leitung endlich repariert ...**
if he comes tomorrow and finally repairs the pipes ...

## Note

- If two infinitive forms occur together with a finite (auxiliary) verb, this latter verb comes first:

**er weiß, dass er es nicht hätte tun sollen**
he knows that he should not have done it

- If a subordinate clause is interrupted by another clause the word order is not affected:

**sie heiratet einen Mann, der, obwohl er nicht reich ist, wenigstens gut aussieht**

she's marrying a man who, although he's not rich, is at least good-looking

## B NEGATIVES

### 1 Main negative words

| | |
|---|---|
| kein, keine, kein *(indef art)* | not a, no |
| keiner, keine, kein(e)s *(pron)* | nobody, none |
| keinerlei | no ... of any sort |
| keineswegs | by no means |
| nicht | not |
| nicht nur ... sondern auch | not only ... but also |
| nicht mehr | no more |
| nichts | nothing |
| nie, niemals | never |
| niemand | nobody |
| nirgends, nirgendwo | nowhere |
| nirgendwohin | (to) nowhere |
| weder ... noch | neither ... nor |

**2** Position of nicht

a) nicht follows the finite verb it refers to:

**ich rauche nicht**　　　　　　　　**du darfst nicht rauchen**
I don't smoke　　　　　　　　　　you're not allowed to smoke

b) If there is an object, nicht follows it:

**er braucht seine Eltern nicht**　　**du hörst mir nicht zu**
he doesn't need his parents　　　　you're not listening to me

**sie hat ihrer Mutter den Brief nicht gegeben**
she didn't give her mother the letter

c) nicht precedes a noun phrase or pronoun if a contrast is involved:

**gib dies nicht deinem Bruder, sondern deiner Schwester**
don't give this to your brother but to your sister

**ich will nicht die blauen Blumen, sondern die gelben**
I don't want the blue flowers, I want the yellow ones

**ich will die gelben Blumen, nicht die blauen**
I want the yellow flowers, not the blue ones

Note that if there is inversion, nicht can occur in more than one position:

**nicht die blauen Blumen will ich, sondern die gelben**
**die blauen Blumen will ich nicht, sondern die gelben**

**3** 'not a', 'not any', 'no' + noun are usually translated by kein-, ie. nicht is not normally used together with ein:

**sie braucht keinen Mann**
she doesn't need a husband

**ich habe keine Reiseschecks**
I haven't got any traveller's cheques

**keine Politesse war zu sehen**
there was no traffic warden in sight

The emphatic 'not a (single)' is translated by kein- einzig-:

**kein einziger Baum blieb stehen**
not a (single) tree was left standing

Note that nicht may occur with ein when ein means one and a contrast is involved:

**sie haben uns nicht eine, sondern zwei Flaschen gebracht**
they have brought us not one, but two bottles

# C DIRECT AND INDIRECT QUESTIONS

## 1 Direct questions

There are four basic ways of forming direct questions in German:

a) *inversion of the normal word order of a statement:*

| **rauchen Sie?** | **schläft sie?** | **regnet es?** |
|---|---|---|
| do you smoke? | is she asleep? | is it raining? |
| **liebst du mich?** | **sprechen Sie Deutsch?** | |
| do you love me? | do you speak German? | |

**darf ich Ihnen meinen Mann vorstellen?**
may I introduce my husband to you?

**ist es letztes Jahr ins Englische übersetzt worden?**
was it translated into English last year?

b) *question word(s) + finite verb (+ subject) (+ complement):*

| wer? | (an) wen? | wessen? | (mit *etc*) wem? |
|---|---|---|---|
| who? | (to) who(m)? | whose? | (with *etc*) whom? |
| wann? | warum? | was? | |
| when? | why? | what? | |
| was für? | welch-? | wie? | |
| what kind of? | which? | how? | |
| wo? | woher? | wohin? | |
| where? | where ... from? | where ... to? | |

*For wo + preposition (eg womit?) see pp 107-08.*

| | |
|---|---|
| **wer kommt?** | **wessen Hut ist das?** |
| who's coming? | whose hat is that? |
| | |
| **mit wem spielt sie?** | **wann geht er?** |
| who is she playing with? | when is he going? |
| | |
| **was siehst du dort?** | **wohin fahren wir?** |
| what do you see there? | where are we going? |
| | |
| **welche Bluse steht mir besser?** | **wie heißt das auf Deutsch?** |
| which blouse suits me better? | what's that in German? |
| | |
| **warum kannst du nicht schlafen?** | |
| why can't you sleep? | |

Note that the case after was für is determined by the preceding preposition or by the following noun's grammatical function, not by the word für:

**bei was für einer Firma arbeitet sie?**
in what kind of firm does she work?

**was für ein Mann könnte so etwas tun?**
what kind of man could do such a thing?

c) *subject + finite verb (+ complement):*

With colloquial questions of this kind, expressing disbelief, the pitch of the voice is raised on the key word, which is also emphasized:

| | |
|---|---|
| ***Oma* tanzt?!** | **Oma *tanzt?!*** |
| *Grandma's* dancing?! | Grandma's *dancing?!* |
| | |
| **das soll *billig* sein?!** | |
| that's supposed to be *cheap*?! | |

d) *subject + finite verb (+ complement) + tag:*

In English there are many question tags, e.g. 'isn't it?', 'aren't you?', 'doesn't he?', 'can't she?', 'wouldn't we?', 'mightn't they?' *etc.* By comparison there are fewer question tags in German.

i) nicht (wahr)?

nicht (wahr)? is normally used at the end of a sentence when confirmation of a statement is expected. It is often shortened to just nicht?, especially in colloquial speech. Only the full form can stand at the beginning of a sentence, though this is uncommon:

**es ist furchtbar kalt heute, nicht (wahr)?**
it's terribly cold today, isn't it?

**nicht wahr, sie gehört in die Mannschaft?**
she should be in the team, shouldn't she?

ja? is an alternative for nicht wahr? at the end of a sentence:

**du kommst heute Abend, ja?**
you're coming this evening, aren't you?

ii) gell?/gelt?

In Southern Germany and Austria gell? or gelt? is frequently found in colloquial speech as an alternative to the above:

**Münchner Bier schmeckt gut, gell?**
Munich beer tastes good, doesn't it?

iii) oder?

oder? at the end of a sentence invites confirmation or a response:

**du isst doch Fleisch, oder?**
you do eat meat, don't you?

**letzten Sonntag haben wir nicht gespielt, oder?**
we didn't play last Sunday, (or) did we?

## 2 Indirect questions

a) *Definition*

Indirect questions follow a verb or a clause and are introduced by an interrogative word, eg:

explain why you're angry
I asked her who she was

b) *Word order*

German word order and punctuation differs from English. The two clauses are always separated by a comma and the finite verb comes at the end of the indirect question.

i) when the 'original' sentence contains an interrogative (eg. wann? warum? was für?):

| | |
|---|---|
| **wann geben Sie Ihr nächstes Konzert?** | → **man fragt, wann Sie Ihr nächstes Konzert geben** |
| when are you going to give your next concert? | people are asking when you are going to give your next concert |
| **warum gefällt es euch nicht?** | → **sagt mal, warum es euch nicht gefällt** |
| why don't you like it? | tell me why you don't like it |
| **was für Kinder unterrichten Sie?** | → **er möchte wissen, was für Kinder Sie unterrichten** |
| what kind of children do you teach? | he wants to know what kind of children you teach |

ii) when the 'original' sentence does not contain an interrogative the indirect question is introduced by ob:

| | |
|---|---|
| **kann er Deutsch?** | → **ich bin gespannt, ob er Deutsch kann** |
| can he speak German? | I'm curious to know if he can speak German |
| **hast du gut geschlafen?** | → **sie hat mich gefragt, ob ich gut geschlafen hätte** |
| did you sleep well? | she asked me if I had slept well |

Note that it is occasionally necessary, as in English, to change the pronouns and the tense (and mood) of the verb in the indirect question from those of the 'original' direct question. *For the correct sequence of tenses see p 149.*

## D ANSWERS ('YES' AND 'NO')

### 1 ja and nein

a) ja means 'yes' and is equivalent to longer positive answers such as: 'yes, it is', 'yes, I will', 'yes, he has' *etc*:

| | |
|---|---|
| **gehst du schon?** | **ja(, ich muss jetzt gehen)** |
| are you going already? | yes(, I have to go now) |

> ## Note
>
> ja can be emphasized in a number of ways:
>
> • by being repeated (ja, ja!)
>
> • in combination with wohl: jawohl! (= 'yes, indeed'), especially in the armed forces

b) nein means 'no' and is equivalent to longer negative answers such as: 'no, it isn't', 'no, I didn't' *etc*:

| | |
|---|---|
| **war es interessant?** | **nein(, es war langweilig)** |
| was it interesting? | no(, it was boring) |

Note that nein and ja used with glauben/denken translate '(don't) think so':

| | |
|---|---|
| **regnet es?** | **ich glaube nein/ich glaube ja** |
| is it raining? | I don't think so/I think so |

## 2 ja or doch?

ja and doch both mean 'yes', but ja is used to answer an affirmative question, and doch to contradict a negative question:

| | | |
|---|---|---|
| **ist dieser Platz frei?** | → | **ja** |
| is this seat taken? | | yes(, it is) |
| **liebst du mich nicht mehr?** | → | **doch** |
| don't you love me any more? | | yes(, I do) |

# 13 TRANSLATION PROBLEMS

## A GENERAL TRANSLATION PROBLEMS

**1** English words not translated in German and vice versa

a) articles

   i) The indefinite article is often left out in German where it is present in English (*see* p 22):

     **er ist leider Popsänger geworden**
     unfortunately he's become a pop singer

   ii) The definite article is often used where it is omitted in English, especially with abstract nouns (*see* p 17):

     **ich verstehe nichts von der Gärtnerei**
     I know nothing about gardening

b) dass and the relative pronoun (*see* p 220 *and* pp 103-07)

These are often omitted in English but must be kept in German:

**er bestand darauf, dass ich komme**
he insisted I come

**das Getränk, das ich am liebsten mag**
the drink I like best

Except for the dass introducing indirect statements, which is optional (*see* p 220):

**er behauptete, dass er krank wäre**
**er behauptete, er wäre krank**
he claimed he was ill

c) After modal verbs a verb expressing motion is very often omitted if there is an adverb or phrase indicating direction (*see* p 161):

**ich muss nach Hause**
I have to go home

**willst du mit ins Kino?**
do you want to come to the cinema?

d) 'can' is sometimes omitted with verbs of perception where it is present in English:

**hörst du mich?**
can you hear me?

**ich spüre nichts**
I can't feel anything

e) German has many adverbs which intensify the meaning of the sentence as a whole. Very often there is no direct, word for word equivalent in English. Common examples are ja, aber, doch, schon, wohl:

**du hast es ja gefunden!**
you've found it!

**das ist aber gescheit!**
that is clever

**das wäre wohl besser**
that would be better

**du verstehst schon?**
you do understand?

## 2 Other differences

a) es

i) es is used as an object with verbs where English has 'so' (*see* p 90):

**du hast es gesagt!**
you said so

**sie hat es getan**
she did so

ii) es is used with sein to refer back to a previous word or clause where there is no equivalent in English:

**sie soll ehrlich sein und sie ist es auch**
she's said to be honest and she is

iii) Note the different word order from English:

**ich bin es**
it's me

Note that 'it' must be translated by er, sie or es depending on the gender of the noun it refers to:

**die Wurst stinkt; willst du sie wirklich essen?**
this sausage smells; do you really want to eat it?

b) *'my', 'you' etc*

The English possessive article (my *etc*) is often translated by the definite article with parts of the body and clothes (*see* p 19):

**wasch dir die Hände!**
wash your hands

**der Hut flog ihm vom Kopf**
his hat flew off his head

c) *commas*

i) In German there are no commas round an adverb within a clause:

**plötzlich fuhr er hoch**
suddenly, he jumped up

**mein Vater wollte natürlich mitspielen**
my father, of course, wanted to join in

ii) A comma is not required:

- when there is a common subject, conjunction or verb which is not repeated:

**er fiel und verstauchte sich den Fuß**
he fell and twisted his ankle

**weil er schneller laufen und also wahrscheinlich gewinnen kann**
because he can run more quickly and can therefore probably win

- before und, aber, oder when the same subject is repeated:

**ich werde ihn sehen und ich werde es ihm sagen**
I will see him and I will tell him

iii) The comma can be omitted when a coordinating conjunction which does not imply a contrast follows a main clause. Thus, main clauses linked by *und* and *oder* no longer need to be preceded by a comma, but can be if this makes the sense clearer:

**Hanna leist ein Buch und Robert spielt Flöte**
Hanna is reading a book and Robert is playing the flute

**er traf sich mit meiner Schwester(,) und deren Freundin war auch mitgekommen**
he met my sister and her friend came along too

The coordinating conjunctions affected by this are: und, oder, beziehungsweise, wie, sowie, weder ... noch, sowohl ... als (auch), entweder ... oder, nicht ... noch.

iv) Commas are still required when a contrasting coordinating conjunction separates main clauses:

**der Stuhl ist alt, aber er ist bequem**
the chair is old but it is comfortable

Contrasting coordinating conjunctions include: aber, doch, jedoch and sondern.

v) Coordinating conjunctions are still preceded by commas when following a subordinate clause:

**er sagte, dass er morgen komme, und fuhr weg**
the said that he would come tomorrow and drove off

vi) Although it is no longer necessary to insert a comma before an infinitival or participial clause, these commas can be retained, particularly when there is a need to stress a separation within the phrase or to avoid confusion:

**sie hatte geplant ins Kino zu gehen**
she had planned to go to the cinema

**sie bot mir(,) ohne einen Augenblick zu zögern(,) ihre Hilfe an**
she offered to help me without a moment's hesitation

*Compare:*

**ich rate, ihm zu helfen**
I advise that you help him

*and:*

**ich rate ihm, zu helfen**
I advise him to help

d) *agreement of subject and verb*

In English, words which are singular in form can have a plural meaning and can be used with either a singular or a plural verb: 'the government thinks/think, the team has/have' *etc.* In German the verb must be singular:

**die Regierung beabsichtigt**    **die Mannschaft hat gewonnen**
the government intend(s)    the team has (have) won

e) *direct speech*

There are various ways of punctuating direct speech in German:

**„du hast recht", sagte sie**
"you're right" she said

*or*

**„du hast recht" sagte sie**

*or*

**„du hast recht", sagte sie**

The last version is mostly used in print.

If 'she said' comes at the beginning then a colon is used with all three options being available:

**sie sagte: „du hast recht"**
she said, "you're right"

A comma must also be used when the quoted words end in a question mark or exclamation mark:

**„was machst du da?", fragte sie**
"what are you doing there?" she asked

**B SPECIFIC TRANSLATION PROBLEMS**

## 1 English verbs ending in -ing

a) As part of a continuous tense these are translated by the appropriate German tense:

| | |
|---|---|
| he's speaking | **er spricht** |
| he was speaking | **er hat gesprochen/er sprach** |
| he had been speaking | **er hatte gesprochen** |
| he will be speaking | **er spricht/er wird sprechen** |
| he would be speaking | **er würde sprechen** |

The first three often have gerade added:
**er spricht gerade** *etc*

b) In German the -ing form is seldom used as a predicative adjective, after the verb, as in: 'he found the film disappointing'. This usage can often be translated by the verb in its finite form:

**der Film enttäuschte ihn**
he found the film disappointing

c) As an adverb, the German usage is often the same as English:

**"ich habe gewonnen!", sagte er lachend**
"I've won", he said, laughing

d) The English -ing form used as a subject or object can often be translated by the German infinitive made into a noun:

**sein Erscheinen überraschte mich**
his coming surprised me

e) An infinitive with zu may also be used:

**das zu sagen bringt uns nicht voran**
saying that won't help

**du solltest versuchen, ihn zu überzeugen**
you should try convincing him

**f)** Very often the -ing structure has to be translated into German by a subordinate clause:

**er lockte die Kunden an, indem er den Preis einiger Artikel senkte**
he attracted customers by lowering the price of a few items

**dadurch, dass sie uns den Raum anbot, hat sie alles ermöglicht**
by offering us the room she made everything possible

**g)** With verbs of perception (seeing, hearing, feeling *etc*), a **wie** clause is common:

**ich beobachte, wie er sich versteckte**
I saw him hiding

**sie fühlte, wie das Kind sich an sie schmiegte**
she felt the child snuggling up to her

**h)** Adverbial phrases of time with a verb in the -ing form very often become a subordinate clause in German:

**bevor er hinausging, schloss er beide Türen ab**
before going out, he locked both doors

**als er die Fußgängerzone überquerte, traf er einen alten Freund**
crossing the pedestrian precinct, he met an old friend

Similar phrases are also often translated by two main clauses joined by **und**:

**er schloss beide Türen sorgfältig ab und ging hinaus**
carefully closing both doors, he went out

**i)** A German relative clause may also be the equivalent of an English phrase with -ing:

**die Polizei sucht eine blonde Frau, die eine grüne Tasche trägt**
the police are looking for a fair-haired woman carrying a green bag

**2** 'there is/are'

a) German usage often avoids direct translation, preferring one of a number of verbs:

**eine Zeitung liegt auf dem Sofa**
there's a newspaper on the sofa

**um die Ecke steht ein Parkhaus**
there's a multi-storey car park round the corner

**überall herrschte Freude**
there was joy everywhere

**ich hätte eine Frage an dich**
there's something I want to ask you

b) es gibt

es gibt is typically used in statements about the fact that something exists (or doesn't exist) in a general sense. It is followed by nouns or pronouns, both singular or plural, in the accusative case. Note also es gab, es hat(te) gegeben, es wird geben *etc*:

**es gibt keine Giftschlangen in Irland**
there are no poisonous snakes in Ireland

**es gab damals wenig zu tun**
there was little to do in those days

**so was gibt es nicht mehr!**
there's no such thing any more!

Note the following idiomatic uses of es gibt:

| | |
|---|---|
| **was gibt's?** | **heute Abend gibt es Milchreis** |
| what's up? | there's rice pudding this evening |

c) es ist, es sind

These are used to indicate presence, often temporary, in a defined space. es ist is followed by a singular and es sind by a plural, both in the nominative case. With inversion es disappears. Note also es war(en) *etc*:

**es ist jemand an der Tür**
there's someone at the door

**es sind Würstchen im Kühlschrank**
there are sausages in the fridge

**Herr Ober, in meiner Suppe ist eine Fliege!**
waiter, there's a fly in my soup!

**in der Stadt war nicht viel los**
there wasn't much happening in town

Note the expression:

**es war einmal ...**
once upon a time ...

## 3 Expressions of place

German distinguishes very precisely whether an expression of place indicates position or motion – and if motion, then whether towards or away from the speaker by attaching either her or hin:

| POSITION | TOWARDS | AWAY FROM |
|---|---|---|
| **wo bist du?** where are you? | **woher kommst du?** where do you come from? | **wohin gehst du?** where are you going? |
| | | **sag mir, wohin du gehst** tell me where you are going |
| **bleib hier!** stay here! | | **geh schnell nach draußen!** go outside quickly! |

**sie bleibt draußen**
she's staying outside

**komm herein!**
come in
**komm hierher!**
come here!

**es ist dort**
it's there
**er ist oben**
he's upstairs
**die Kirche steht links**
the church is on the
left
**es ist innen schon
gestrichen**
it's already been
painted inside
**sie warten schon
drinnen**
they're waiting inside
**sie sitzt hinten**
she's sitting at the
back

**komm nach oben!**
come upstairs!

**es kommt dorthin!**
it goes there

**dann gehen Sie nach
links**
then you go left
**die Tür geht nach
innen auf**
the door opens
inwards

**er ging nach hinten**
he went to the back

## 4 'to put'

German very often translates 'to put' by a more specific verb
indicating precisely how the object is put, i.e. whether it is set
down, laid down *etc*:

a) legen means the object lies:

**sie legte ihre Hand auf seinen Kopf**
she put her hand on his head

**er legte die Zeitung auf den Stuhl**
he put the newspaper on the chair

b) setzen means the object sits:

**er setzte das Kind aufs Töpfchen**
he put the child on the potty

Note also:

**hier musst du ein Komma setzen**
you have to put a comma here

c) stecken means the object goes inside something:

**er steckte den Schlüssel ins Schloss**
he put the key in the lock

**der Spion steckte die Papiere ins Geheimfach**
the spy put the papers in the secret compartment

**sie steckten ihn für drei Jahre ins Gefängnis**
they put him in prison for three years

d) stellen means the object stands:

**er stellte die Milch in den Kühlschrank**
he put the milk into the fridge

**wir haben den Mahagonitisch ins Wohnzimmer gestellt**
we've put the mahogany table in the living room

e) tun is the most general term for 'to put'; it is slightly colloquial:

**er tat das Geld schnell in die Tasche**
he quickly put the money in his pocket

**tun Sie das bitte wieder weg**
put it away again, please

## 5 'all the'

'all the' followed by a singular noun is usually translated by ganz
rather than all der *etc*:

**die ganze Mannschaft**
all the team

**das ganze Geld**
all the money

## 6 The passive

The passive tends to be less common in German than in English. It is often replaced by man:

> **das tut man nicht**
> that isn't done

> **man behauptet, er habe das Geld gestohlen**
> he is said to have stolen the money

lassen can be used with an infinitive which has a passive sense (see p 145):

> **das lässt sich machen**
> that can be done

> **ich lasse das Zimmer neu tapezieren**
> I'm having the room repapered

The active form with the agent (by ...) as the subject is often used:

> **viele hielten Pele für den besten Fußballspieler der Welt**
> Pele was believed by many to be the best footballer in the world

## 7 'when'

a) For a single event in the future: wenn

> **wenn ich bald nach New York fliege, nehme ich dich mit**
> when I fly to New York soon I'll take you with me

> **wenn wir in Zukunft nichts zu tun haben, ruhen wir uns aus**
> in future, when we have nothing to do we're going to relax

b) For a repeated action or state in the present, past or future: wenn

> **wenn er abends Hunger hat, isst er immer Erdnüsse**
> when(ever) he's hungry in the evening he always eats peanuts

> **wenn die Sonne schien, pflegten wir im Freien zu spielen**
> whenever the sun shone we used to play out of doors

c) For a single event in the past: als

**als wir euch zum ersten Mal sahen, bekamen wir einen Schock**
when we saw you for the first time we got a shock

**als ich sechs Jahre alt war, konnte ich noch nicht lesen**
when I was six I still couldn't read

d) For questions: wann

**wann war das?**
when was that?

**wann gehst du endlich ins Bett?**
when are you eventually going to go to bed?

**ich möchte wissen, wann du endlich ins Bett gehst**
I'd like to know when you're eventually going to go to bed

Note that in indirect statements, wann is used following verbs
of saying and many similar verbs, even if a question is not
implied:

**er hat mir erzählt, wann er die Entdeckung machte**
he told me when he made the discovery

**ich habe vergessen, wann er sie getroffen hat**
I have forgotten when he met her

# INDEX

**E**

**F**